Rising Above the Storms of Life

RISING ABOVE
THE STORMS OF LIFE

Handling Our Emotions God's Way

MARY PYTCHES

eagle

Guildford, Surrey

British Library Cataloguing in Publication Data. A catalogue record for this book is available from the British Library.

Published by Eagle, an imprint of Inter Publishing Service (IPS) Ltd, PO Box 530, Guildford, Surrey GU2 5FH.

Typeset by Eagle
Printed by Cox & Wyman
ISBN No: 0 86347 375 X

CONTENTS

INTRODUCTION

No one likes to feel angry, resentful, anxious or depressed for long. However, sometimes these feelings don't disappear with a word of command. They may be due to an illness, difficult circumstance or other people's insensitivity, but often it is just a reaction we have to a situation which is not the way we personally would like to have it. Whatever the cause, negative feelings drain our energy, distract us from more important issues and cry out to be eased.

The purpose of this book is to find ways of dealing with these uncomfortable and unwelcome emotions. Understanding our feelings and the triggers for them is where we begin. Although understanding alone will not bring relief, it is a good place to start and provides ideas of how to proceed. Unfinished business from the past may be provoking the difficult feelings, or it may be a present situation. In both cases action is needed. Changing our circumstances may be a way forward but when that is not possible then there are only two options left to us; to change our behaviour or our attitude.

While I am aware that I don't possess all the answers, I hope the suggestions in this book for dealing with unwelcome emotions will assist any who, at times, feel as if they are in a losing battle with negative feelings.

As usual I have to thank my husband, David, who hovers over my manuscripts with a red pen while I hold my breath. His suggestions, and the illustrations he finds me, are invaluable. While I write the house gets dusty, the food gets scanty and the meals get scrappy, but he continues to be patient, showing amazing forbearance. I am grateful to my friend, Dr John Cowan, who kindly found the time to check some of the medical terminology, to make sure I didn't make a complete fool of myself! Thanks also to my son-in-law, Chris Cocksworth, who now and again found he had 'mail waiting' when I would anxiously e-mail him a page or two to double check for abstruse theological errors. I am grateful to all my family and friends for their encouragement and interest.

One

WEATHERING THE STORM

Anyone who has read Carol Wimber's delightful book, *The Way It Was*, describing the life of her husband, John, must have wondered, as I did, how they coped? Carol details some of John's suffering; the emotional pain of time and again having his good called evil, the pain of knowing that his eldest son, Chris, was dying of a brain tumour, his own physical trauma from cancer treatment, the physical sense of imbalance that remained after a stroke and the final urgent need for bypass surgery.

The constant criticism would have been enough for the most stoic. For example, when they were finally asked to leave their beloved Friend's Church, they went with the church's blessing, but some fledgling Baptist church a few miles away gave out flyers saying that John had been expelled from the Friends for gross immorality. In fact they were released when the Spirit began to move upon about forty of the members and the church preferred to let them go before more of their members were 'infected'. On other occasions he received death threats, and once in a restaurant a man attacked him shouting, 'Antichrist, Antichrist'. John quickly left the restaurant. Criticism was a constant occurrence. How did the Wimbers rise above the suffering and persevere in their wide ministry almost to the end of John's life?[1]

Thank God not all of us have to pass through such

intense times of trial. But pain is part and parcel of life. 'Man is born to trouble as sparks fly upwards.'[2] Which means that none of us will escape some suffering during our lifetime. Barbara Johnson says that Christians are Easter People living in a Good Friday world.[3] This means pain is part of living, but it also implies that in some measure we should be experiencing something of the Easter triumph alongside the suffering. Although at times we do, nevertheless we are often plagued, not just by difficult events, but by the hard-to-manage feelings that the events stimulate.

One of the hardest challenges in life is how to handle our feelings. These may be the secret emotions which fester beneath the surface of our lives, erupting at times to cause trouble. One young man told me he ruined many of his relationships because he was often angry. A girl said she never remembered a day of her life when she had woken up glad to be alive. Another woman told me that several times a year she would sink into a depression which came on unexpectedly and lasted several weeks.

More often the painful feelings are caused by difficult circumstances or the thoughtlessness and insensitivity of others. This is particularly difficult when those who cause the pain are people who are significant to us, members of our family, our church or our work. Then there are the difficult circumstances of loss, whether it be loss of a loved one, friends, home, community, job, home group, church, pet, even a possession. In these circumstances we struggle to keep our emotional equilibrium.

Henri Nouwen has published a private journal he kept during a time of deep emotional pain when a close relationship ended. He writes,

That was a time of extreme anguish, during which I wondered whether I would be able to hold on to my life. Everything came crashing down – my self-esteem, my energy to live and work, my sense of being loved, my hope for healing, my trust in God . . . everything. Here I was, a writer about the spiritual life, known as someone who loves God and gives hope to people, flat on the ground and in total darkness.[4]

He says that at that time he came face to face with his own nothingness and could see nothing in front of him but a bottomless pit.

The question I want to ask is this: 'As Christians how do we handle the painful feelings which often enter our lives as unwelcome guests?'

The American personal growth course, Free to Be,[5] states that emotional maturity is understanding what a feeling is, accepting feelings as a unique gift of God, identifying and confessing feelings, both hard and good ones, owning one's own feelings, understanding that there are no right or wrong feelings, and lastly learning to express feelings appropriately. Then comes the impacting sentence: 'What a person does with feelings decides emotional maturity.' All of this I would agree with, but in my experience the real problem lies in the last sentence. What do we do with the spontaneous, unbidden feelings which we do not want to harbour and certainly do not want to act out in any ungodly manner, but will not go away? When a difficult situation is unchanging these unwanted feelings are continually stimulated. Life can be difficult and often we are tormented by an emotional reaction to our circumstances; a reaction which can be unwelcome, very wearing, and stubbornly resistant to change. We do all the right things; we confess, we acknowledge, we forgive, we lay it down. The next day we awake only to find the torture is back. Then it is only too easy to mismanage our feelings and fall into a variety of traps commonly associated with painful emotions.

Trap 1 – Suppression

The most frequently used method of dealing with emotions is to suppress them. In fact children are often taught and encouraged to handle their emotions in this way because it is the most grown-up thing to do. How many children are told not to cry when they are hurt because they are a 'big boy or girl now'? This is a common route especially for Christians. Rather than be an ordinary human being they try to be super-spiritual and show only 'good' feelings to the public. They may even be told by their church to be joyful. Barbara Johnson quotes from a lady whose two children died very tragically. 'When our children died, everyone kept telling us to rejoice. We tried to, and in the interim I denied the reality of my grief and now I'm unable to cry, so the only emotion that comes from me is anger . . . I am so uptight right now I feel like a pressure cooker about to explode.'[6]

One elderly lady told me that she didn't have time to grieve her husband's death. She said she had too much to do and too many people to look after. But in the subsequent weeks she 'still refused to indulge', as she would put it, in her sadness. Gradually her health began to deteriorate, she became depressed and disinclined to go anywhere. On the anniversary of her husband's death she was a sick woman. It may appear a Christian thing to do, but suppression is not a healthy way forward. According to Susan Jeffers, acknowledgement of pain is very important; denial is deadly. 'Pain can be incredibly destructive if kept submerged . . . unacknowledged pain is subtly destroying many people's lives.'[7] 'The goal is balance, not emotional suppression: every feeling has its value and significance.'[8]

Two major reasons why people swallow their feelings are shame and fear. We are either of the opinion that it is not right for a Christian to experience certain emotions, or we are afraid that by admitting to something painful we would be opening up Pandora's box. Many people subconsciously know that they have buried painful incidents from the past. There is a natural fear of what they might uncover if they were once to start saying how they really felt. So any hint of sorrow, anger or fear is quickly choked back, swallowed and suppressed.

Suppression and denial go hand in hand. We suppress our feelings and with our words deny that anything is wrong. Perhaps we think there is too much to lose if we admit to being unhappy, angry or anxious, so we pretend that all is well. A person in denial says that things are fine, or getting better, when they may even be getting worse or have certainly not improved. The consequences of facing reality may be too awful to contemplate, so we bury our heads in the sand. It reminds me of the Hans Christian Anderson story of the king whose tailor made him an invisible suit of clothes, and somehow persuaded him that even though he was absolutely naked, he was actually finely dressed. No one was prepared to disagree with the king, for fear of losing their heads, so his courtiers and citizens all agreed with His Royal Highness that he was indeed wonderfully dressed. So he walked around stark naked, tricked into thinking he was fully clothed, aided and abetted by a population prepared to live in denial for fear of the consequences. Suddenly a small child, who had not yet learned to lie, spoke up – the only one prepared to say what everyone else knew but were too afraid to admit, that the king was 'as naked as the day that he was born'.

One of the tragedies of the now defunct Nine O'clock Service(NOS) in Sheffield was that, though many of the members must have been aware that all was not well, and that their leader was manipulative and abusive, no one said a word. They had invested so much of their lives in the vision and could not face the personal loss of admitting to such a thing. Two young women eventually blew the whistle and the truth came out. It was denial by the vast majority of the membership which had kept the truth hidden for so long.

One of the most baffling forms of denial is when a person ignores symptoms of a life-threatening illness. They refuse to visit a doctor for fear of being told bad news. They bolster themselves up by telling themselves, 'It's really nothing,' or 'It's just indigestion,' and sadly may leave the situation too late to be helped.

One of the results of suppression and denial is that we begin to lose our real selves. We cease to be authentic people and become masks of unreality. This is not to say that there is no place for self-control; it is an important fruit of the Spirit, but there is a difference between suppression and self-control. In the former the feeling never sees the light of day. Instead it is buried alive and we begin slowly to die to our feeling self.

In the latter the feeling is admitted but expressed

appropriately.

Although feelings of anger are normal it is an especially unwelcome emotion. Many Christians think that it is wrong to be angry, or even to feel angry. When we swallow anger we either end up with high blood pressure, or explode over some innocent person who has done nothing to warrant our pent-up emotion. This is an inappropriate expression of our feelings which can be another trap.

Trap 2 – Inappropriate Expression

Sadness, anger, fear, all such feelings need an outlet, but that outlet should be appropriate in terms of time and place, which is to exercise self-control. While living in Chile, when we suffered earthquakes it was natural to be afraid, but it was not appropriate to show this in front of the children. While they were with us we had to appear calm. Afterwards we could express our feelings to one another! My husband has a very good way of handling anger. If someone upsets him he immediately writes a letter saying exactly what he thinks. The next day he tears it up and writes a calmer one. He gets his feelings out of his system, but harms no one. In fact he probably waits a week before finally responding, by which time he can see things calmly and in better perspective.

Paul told the Ephesian Christians to be angry but not to sin.[9] So it is not anger that is wrong, it is the way in which we express it. Jesus was certainly angry with the money-changers in the temple and expressed that indignation in no uncertain terms and yet Jesus was without sin. The deciding factors which makes anger right or wrong are the motivation behind it and the way it is expressed. Anger should be expressed appropriately and not violently which is such a common reaction today. Violence is on the increase both on our streets and in our homes. Children are brought up in families where violence is commonplace, not only between the adults around them, but daily on the television. The recent massacre of school children in Little Rock, Arkansas by a fellow student, shocked the world. Soon after there was a copy-cat killing in Tabor, Canada and another in Texas; in each they shot their peers. This was anger gone berserk. Anger is a painful emotion and when we do not know how to express it appropriately then it festers away, and eventually explodes and causes damage.

In today's pressurised world stress, anger and frustration are growing problems. A recent survey suggests that an estimated 302,000 people in Britain reported suffering from work-related stress and a further 261,000 reported that they believed themselves to be suffering from a 'stress-related' condition.[10] Men and women are under pressure to perform or lose their jobs. There is a dread of redundancy. An increased work load requires excessive hours. Failure to meet dead-lines could mean the loss of a contract. As a result of increasing stress many former relatively safe places, safe at least from other humans, are becoming dangerous. In the air passengers feel helpless. Recently planes have had to be diverted, or a passenger restrained, because of uncontrollable anger which has terrified the others on board. Road rage is becoming a common occurrence. Now it is computer rage. What will the next 'rage' be? Men and women are so frustrated and full of anger that many are taking time to attend anger or stress management seminars. In a centre for violent men there was a man who had slapped his girlfriend and smashed her window with his bare fist. Another had wrapped a telephone cord around his wife's neck. A husband had been imprisoned for manslaughter, after his release he decided to clean up his act, but then he started working long hours and the obsessiveness of his personality began to take hold again. The stress spilled over and he suddenly became violent again, nearly killing his wife. On one occasion he threw her across a courtyard, pinned her to the wall and punched her in the face. It was at this point he sought help from the centre.11

This is the pressurised world we live in. Nor are Christians exempt from the same strains. We suffer the same stresses as everyone else, and in too many instances react to the pressure in the same angry way.

Trap 3 – Inertia

I recently received a letter from a young woman who had suffered a nervous breakdown. She was off work for several months and during that time received some counselling. There were good reasons for her stress-related illness, but the cause of her breakdown lay in her doing nothing about the increasing signs of stress – her growing depression, inability to concentrate and sleeplessness. Many people suffer from symptoms of stress, and do nothing about them until they are so sick that only drastic action can help. My young friend might well have avoided the breakdown in health had she heeded the warning signs which had plagued her for at least a year.

So often it is shame which hinders us from seeking help. A middle-age man confessed that he had suffered from a limiting anxiety disorder for twenty years and had told no one because he was so ashamed of his weakness. We incorrectly think that Christians should be above such afflictions and that their presence is a sign of failure on our part, or God's.

Trap 4 – Blame Shifting

Another trap we sometimes fall into is blaming others or blaming God. Others may have caused us the problem and the pain, but our reaction is our responsibility. No one can make us 'feel' in any certain way. The woman who had the nervous breakdown blamed a selfish, inconsiderate land-lord for her ill health. It was true he had been a major cause of her stress, but she had failed to act in a sensible way to deal with the situation. It was her inaction which led to her breakdown, not her landlord. Sadly in these sort of situations action is often easier said than done. Stress leads on to depression which acts like a paralysis. Decisions are hard to make, self-confidence is at a low ebb, and so we do nothing. It is then easy to blame others and sometimes even God. Why did he not protect me, or those I love? Why did he send this trial? If he is God, surely he could have stopped it? Understandable questions to ask, but we need to take another look at the Scriptures. Paul was an amazing missionary. He was the apostle to the Gentiles and yet he suffered terrible trials, physically, emo-tionally, mentally and spiritually. Jesus was God's only Son, and he died on a cross in agony, deserted by his friends and for a while abandoned by his Father. The tri-als and difficulties which come our way are certainly not a failure on God's part. The only failure in the experience may be in the way we deal with the resulting feelings.

As we continue down this road it is easy to become a permanent 'victim'. A victim is a person who has given the control of his life to someone else. When we live in blame we give the other person power to control how we feel. In Victor Frankl's inspiring classic, *Man's Search for Meaning*, he asks himself, as a prisoner, if his reaction to the singular world of the concentration camp proves that man cannot escape the influences of his surroundings. 'Does man have no choice of action in the face of such circumstances?' His experience of the Nazi concentration camp proved to Victor Fankl that man did have a choice of action. The conclusion he came to was that in such a place everything could be taken away from a man but one thing – the last of the human freedoms – to choose one's attitude in any given set of circumstances – to choose one's own way. He says that it is this spiritual freedom – which cannot be taken away – that makes life meaningful and purposeful.[12]

This truth was amazingly illustrated by the Rev Dale Lang's reaction to the copycat killing of his young seventeen-year-old son, Jason, in a Tabor high school in Canada. Coming so soon after the killings in Littleton, Colorado, it shocked not only the local community, but the wider world who learned of it through the news media. An article in a Calgary newspaper written by Rick Bell expresses surprise at Rev Lang's reaction.

> I'm sure I'm not alone in feeling a little unease, a twitch of the spirit, a sense of not measuring up, as we all listen and watch Rev Dale Lang. Here is a man, flesh and blood and heart, just like the rest of us. His teenage boy, Jason, is gunned down and killed. Just last week. And what does he do? Does Rev Lang blame the government, the school, the accused, somebody, anybody? Does he vow revenge? Does he lament a cruel universe? Does he

call the shrinks, head to a talk show or try to find himself? No, Rev Lang speaks and prays and acts with the confidence of a man of faith. He hurts. There's no doubt about that. You can see it when he speaks of Jason's Z28 Camaro with the T-roof. Jason got his dream car a couple of days before he died. Dad signed the loan and, on the morning of Jason's death, Rev Lang taught his son how to use the stickshift. The For Sale sign's imprint can still be seen on the rear window and the T-roof is open, the way Jason liked. You can hear the pain when Rev Lang tells all of us he must now go to his boy's bedroom where nothing has been touched since the shooting. His voice breaks. And that's where most stories stop. Death and grief. But the Anglican cleric is a man of faith. Rev Lang knows his son is with God. He believes there is something called the will of God, something more than mortgages, promotions and the swankiest vehicle on the block. It is crystal clear, for Rev Lang, that life is far more than a game where the person with the most toys wins. Yes, this week Rev Lang asks us not to look outside and point fingers or shift responsibility. He wants us to look inside. This is a dangerous thing to do in these times. Some of us don't know if there's anything on the inside. 'I don't want my son's death to be a random act of violence that leaves us scarred,' says Rev Lang. 'I don't want Jason's death to be meaningless. I want his death to count for something.'

The Rev Dale Lang and his family were the victims of

violence, but he did not possess a victim mentality. He refused to let the gunman have the last word. It would have been so easy for him to have blamed others for what happened. But blaming is a dead-end road. It leads nowhere, except to despair and hopelessness.

Most of us have taken one of these routes in our attempts to deal with difficult and painful feelings. We have lived in a world where it is thought normal to suppress our feelings; to express them inappropriately; to do nothing until we break apart, or blame others. The fact is most of us have had no teaching on healthy ways of handling our feelings.

A few years ago we visited the Vasa Museum in Stockholm. The *Vasa* dates back to 1628 and was Gustav II Adolf's warship which sank in the middle of Stockholm's harbour on its maiden voyage. Following extensive underwater exploration, the *Vasa* was finally located and salvaged in 1961 after having been in the water for 333 years. Apparently, with crowds watching, the then King of Sweden's pride and joy sank just a short distance from the harbour. A powerful gust of wind caught the canvas sails and she keeled over – righted herself and then keeled over to port, sinking swiftly in 110 feet of water. It was a major catastrophe. One of the largest naval vessels of the age had gone to the bottom in her own harbour under peaceful conditions and on her maiden voyage. Why? Because she was top-heavy. The builders had failed to put in sufficient ballast for the number of decks, two of them with heavy cannons.

In the early years of our missionary service in South America we used to travel by sea. Passing down the Bay of Biscay it was always a relief to us that modern-day ships are built with good stabilisers. Not because we were afraid of sinking like the *Vasa*, but because when the sea became rough, these kept the ship on a fairly even keel, and modified the risk of sea-sickness.

When the wind of adversity blows upon our lives we need good ballast, or firm stabilisers to keep us on an emotionally even keel. In adversity our feelings can be so strong as to make us feel that, like the *Vasa*, we are about to capsize, or at least become extremely sick! Where then can we find sufficient ballast or adequate stabilisers to rise above the storms of life and not to sink beneath the waves?

The Bible is an amazingly practical book. Although it does not have a chapter which spells out 'How to deal with difficult feelings', there are very obvious clues across its pages. But first, however, we must try to understand the subject we are dealing with. Before going into battle an army commander studies his enemy until he understands him thoroughly. Though I hasten to add that our emotions are not the enemy, even if at times they might seem that way. It will help us, nevertheless, to handle them if we understand them better.

A Personal Review

- How do you usually handle your negative emotions?
- If your tendency is to suppress them, what causes you to do this?
- How would you describe emotional maturity?

Two

WHAT IS AN EMOTION?

Before we examine some biblical ways of handling our emotions we need to understand them and how they are triggered.

How Our Brain Functions

In Daniel Goleman's book *Emotional Intelligence* he takes emotion to refer to a feeling and its distinctive thoughts, psychological and biological states and range of propensities to act.[1] By this definition he appears to link emotions and thoughts together, leading sometimes to action. It is sometimes hard to distinguish our feelings from our thoughts, but most cognitive therapists would suggest that our thinking leads to feelings which then lead to action. For example: Two men may be made redundant on the same day. The first drives home excited and happy, to tell his wife. The second drives around for hours contemplating suicide and afraid of going home. The fact of redundancy had triggered a thought process within both the men. The first imagined the redundancy money he would be getting and how he would spend it to set himself up in business. These thoughts stimulated his happiness. The other man, on hearing the news, was reminded of all the other failures in his life and now added this redundancy to that list. These thoughts produced feelings of increasing sadness and depression.

It is true that in many cases our thinking does trigger feelings and feelings can then lead to action. However, it would seem from Goleman that it is not quite as tidy as that neat thesis would imply. In his view there is a sense in which we have two minds – one that thinks and one that feels. The rational mind is the one we are most conscious of, because it makes us more aware, thoughtful and able to ponder and reflect. The other system of knowing, the emotional mind, is more impulsive and powerful and sometimes illogical.[2] My husband, David, will sometimes tell others how irritating it is to be told something by his wife that she has no explanation for – she just knows! 'She is illogical,' he will say, 'but often irritatingly right.' Despite this admission of irritation, when talking to church leaders he will encourage them to pray and 'go with their gut feelings' when it comes to leading their churches in the things of the Spirit. And as he says it he acknowledges the importance of emotional intelligence – the knowing we get through our feelings.

It would seem that the knowing mind and the emotional mind act in a very close-knit way, though our western civilisation has tended to elevate the rational mind and disregarded the feelings as 'just emotions – not to be trusted'. The thrust of Goleman's book is to change this mindset and to show us the importance of understanding our emotions so that we can manage and use them better. To back this up he gives us a clear description of how the brain works. For those with a scientific bent it is a fascinating book. However, for most of us a simple explanation will suffice.

Emotions are a Response

Apparently, the root of our passions lies in the limbic system, a part of the brain that surrounds the brain stem. In the limbic system are two almond-shaped clusters called the amygdala. They lie one each side of the brain, towards the side of the head. The amygdala are our emotional memory bank. They are specialists when it comes to emotions. The sensory organs; eyes, ears, nose etc. send signals to the brain. There are then two pathways these signals can travel, which will give us either a feeling response, or a thinking response. The signals can bypass the thinking part of the brain, called the neocortex and go straight to the amygdala which leads to a feeling response. A woman walking down a dark alley at night, on hearing footsteps behind her doesn't think about being afraid and then quicken her footsteps, she immediately reacts to what she has heard; she feels afraid and walks faster.

The second pathway the signals can travel is straight to the neocortex, or the thinking brain and from there to the amygdala. In this case there is a more deliberate response which has been thought through. A young couple were looking at houses to buy. They saw one in an area they were particularly attracted to; it was right in every way except for the kitchen. This was much too small for their growing family and for the entertaining they hoped to do. The wife immediately assumed it was no good. Hers was more of a feeling response than a thinking one. The husband on the other hand looked at the house and thought about the situation. He viewed it from this angle and that. His thinking was: 'Shall we lose an attractive house, in an area we like just because the kitchen is too small? Perhaps we can manage for a while and then, when we have the money extend the kitchen.' His was a thoughtful response and in fact he was able to win his wife over. They now live in a delightful house, very suited to their needs, with an extended kitchen.

Controlling Our Emotions

The rational mind does not decide what emotions we 'should' have, nor when we should have them. Feelings usually come to us as a *fait accompli*. What the rational mind can do is control the course of those reactions. With a few exceptions, we do not decide when to be mad, sad or glad etc. But what we do with those feelings is controllable by the thinking mind.[3] On one of our leaves from Chile we were lent a house near a railway line. Rationally I am well aware that in England one is unlikely to experience a major earthquake. Nevertheless, every time a train rumbled down the track, resembling the sound of an earthquake, I would stiffen in fear. In an instant my adrenaline prepared me for action. The sound alone triggered my anxiety and only after the feeling had surfaced would I talk to myself, calling on my rational mind to come to my aid. I would tell myself that I was in fact back in England which rarely, if ever, suffers from earthquakes. Diving under the table would, therefore, be unnecessary!

'All emotions are, in essence, impulses to act.'[4] Our feelings can be dangerous when we fail to control our actions. They can then have devastating consequences. We have all encountered tragic family situations where a husband and father decides to leave his wife and family because he has become romantically attached to another woman. That wonderful feeling of love has been allowed to spill over the boundaries that God has set for our protection and happiness. Maintaining appropriate boundaries in all our relationships is vital. It is easy to deceive ourselves and think we can play with fire and still control it. The only safe option is to stay within the limits. Falling in love can be an overwhelming feeling and once it has happened it is more difficult to extract oneself by using rational self-talk.

A team of Italian psychiatrists have discovered striking biological similarities between people who are lovesick and sufferers of obsessive compulsive disorder. OCD is a mental illness characterised by obsessive intrusive thoughts. A person with this condition feels compelled to repeat mundane activities, such as washing hands or checking that doors are locked. Donatella Marazziti, a psychiatrist at the University of Pisa, carried out research which showed that OCD was linked with low levels of a chemical called serotonin. Apparently both OCD sufferers and those in love had about 40 per cent less serotonin than normal.[5] If this is true then it would be wise to exercise self-control in the earlier stages of an illicit attraction rather than later when the attachment has become a compulsion.

In a society of 'anything goes so long as it fulfils you and makes you happy', self-control is not a popular concept. Sadly this cultural mind-set has even infiltrated the Christian church and we hear little about self-control, which is one of the fruits of the Spirit. On a recent training day for people wanting to learn how to minister to others a woman asked what she should do if she was suddenly taken with a desire to intercede publicly when she was in the middle of a one-to-one prayer ministry. I gathered that she did not mean just a desire to pray, but a loud intercessory crying. I said quite simply that she should finish ministering to the person and then take herself off somewhere else and intercede. She looked surprised by my lack of sympathy and said that she would not be able to control it. But Scripture tells us that the spirit of the prophet is subject to the prophet. In other words the gifts of the Spirit can be exercised in a controlled way. But she didn't agree. So I suggested that she was probably not called to be on a ministry team but to intercession. If she was not able to exercise appropriate self-control she should stay in her room and intercede privately. To me it was an illustration of how easily the church has been contaminated by the cultural norms around it.

Part of self-control is self-awareness. This is the ability to step back from an experience for a moment, and recognise the feeling the experience generates. Self-control is deciding what one does with that feeling. Occasionally one is bothered by a fleeting, rather nebulous feeling of disquiet. It doesn't appear to be connected to an experience. A self-aware person will soon be able to put a name to the feeling, and from there be able to find the cause. A young friend worked for several months on her quick temper. As she grew more self-aware she was able to recognise the feeling of irritation before it spiralled into anger and hurtful words. Soon she found herself able to sense the irritation, quickly find the cause and before the anger flared was able to choose a more thoughtful response.

Emotions Can Appear Irrational

As we all know we can, at times, be mystified by our feelings. They can appear illogical and unjustified. They may even be overwhelming in their intensity. Sometimes they seem to have a mind of their own. One of the facts worth noting about the amygdala is that it is almost mature at birth in the human baby, whereas the thinking part of the brain develops much more slowly. Which means emotional memory begins at a very early age before the baby can reason about what is happening. This is why we can sometimes be bothered by inexplicable feelings that seem to have no logical reason for being there. It is possible to have an emotional memory of something which happened before our mind was capable of rational thought. I once prayed for a lady who suffered from claustrophobia. She found any small, enclosed space difficult to handle. We asked God to show her the reason for this fear and eventually he did. We were praying one afternoon and she suddenly felt as if she were in a very tight place. She felt constricted as if in a rabbit warren. She then began to struggle as if trying to escape. When the struggle was eventually over we came to the conclusion that she had been reliving what had apparently been a difficult birth experience. She checked with her mother during the next week and learned that she had indeed had a difficult birth as a war baby born during an air-raid. What is more, when she came back to see us the following week she announced that the claustrophobic feelings had disappeared. This is not to say that every case of claustrophobia is due to a difficult birth, nor that everyone is healed that easily.

Another difficulty with our emotional memory is that it may be out of date. It has a tendency to respond to situations inappropriately because it has confused a present situation with something similar from the past and responded as if it were the same, whereas there may be only faint similarities. This is why the emotional circuit is sloppy and unreliable on its own. It may act before there is full confirmation. As Goleman says: 'It frantically commands that we react to the present in ways that were imprinted long ago, with thoughts, emotions, reactions learned in response to events perhaps only dimly similar.'[6] Someone I once knew was terrified of men. She would break out in a sweat if she was left alone with someone of the opposite sex. She was, at the time, a woman of twenty-five, but was reacting to a situation of sexual abuse which had happened when she was five. Another person reacted very ungraciously to a friend coming into her kitchen and giving her a helping hand by putting away her dishes. On being asked what was wrong she was at first bewildered, but on thinking it over said it made her feel as if she was being controlled, just as she had been as a child, by an older bossy sister.

For these two reasons alone we might be tempted to think that we should never trust our emotions. However, emotions may be irrational but they are not unreasonable. We may not understand them at first but if we do a little digging we usually find there is good reason for them.

Emotions Are Varied

As we later will examine what triggers our emotions, we first need a description of these emotions themselves. There are a myriad feelings which touch the human heart in the course of a lifetime. I have condensed them into eight major ones. To my mind most others are derivatives of these eight. Four are positive and four are negative. Mostly we will focus on the negative feelings being the most difficult to handle. However, even positive feelings can run riot in our lives occasionally and need to be restrained.

Four Positive Emotions	**Four Negative Emotions**
Love	Anger
Hope	Anxiety
Peace	Guilt
Joy	Sadness

Of these eight there are many derivations.
- Love – fondness, friendship, affection, devotion, passion
- Hope – anticipation, expectation, longing, optimism
- Peace – confidence, assurance, faith, calmness, concord, tranquillity
- Joy – happiness, satisfaction, gladness, delight, rapture, pleasure, contentment

- Anger – frustration, resentment, fury, rage, hostility, animosity, hatred
- Anxiety – fear, worry, pre-occupation, panic, dread
- Guilt – self-condemnation, self-consciousness, remorse, contrition, shame
- Sadness – loneliness, misery, depression, distress, grief, anguish, dejection, woe, melancholy.

Negative Emotions

Although we would all rather not experience the negative emotions, only a stony heart could watch the evening news and never feel sadness or anger, even guilt, at the horrible plight of thousands of people fleeing their worn torn countries around the world. However, the problem arises when we allow negative emotions to continue for longer than is healthy, even godly, without taking appropriate action to deal with them.

Many know, to their cost, the suffering which can

result from the stress of living with a prolonged negative emotion. 'Emotions that wax too intensely or for too long – undermine our stability.'[7] As the stress levels soar in the manic world of the twenty-first century it is imperative that we find ways of managing our emotions in healthy ways.

Maturity is not, as is mistakenly thought by some, not having strong emotions. It is experiencing feelings, both good and bad, understanding those feelings and making sure we have the ballast and the stabilisers in our lives that will prevent us being overwhelmed by the painful and difficult ones.

Simple understanding does not heal us. It just makes us more informed neurotics! However, on our journey towards wholeness we all need a place to start and so we must start with our understanding. The theory of our emotions is part of the process of discovery. The next step is knowing some of the trigger points for our feelings.

Review

1. Which is your most likely response to what happens to you, a 'feeling' one or a 'rational' one?
2. Describe any experience you may have had when you have failed to exercise appropriate self-control. What could you have done instead?
3. Do you ever experience feelings which seem irrational? Where do you think they may come from?

Three

TRIGGER POINTS

It is important not to run away from our difficult feelings. 'The discomfort is a signal, a teacher offering us a valuable lesson.'[1] We may think the difficult feelings are evil and should be suppressed quickly, or that they are illogical and best ignored. But that would be to miss the lesson such feelings can teach us. There is a good reason for them. Knowing what that reason is will help us to deal with them appropriately and, for some of us, unlock a whole new area of growth.

Circumstances and Events

Troublesome feelings may be caused by events or circumstances, either past or present. It is hard to divorce the past from the present. Especially when the way we react to present events is often determined by past experiences. On the surface it may appear to be a present event that is triggering the difficult feelings, but something in the past may be amplifying the feelings — something long since forgotten, but stored by our emotional memory. As we have already seen it may only dimly resemble the present circumstance. Or it may even be something which happened to us before our rational mind was developed, since our emotional memory may be able to store up the feelings from the womb. A young girl I know was separated from her mother at birth. After several months she was adopted and has grown up to be a healthy, happy adult, except that she has an inordinate fear of separation and death. She appears to over-react emotionally at the first sign of any lengthy separation from her family. It seems illogical until one learns of her early history.

Talking, over the years, to hundreds of people about their problems I am more convinced than ever that the formative years between 0–18 are decisive in laying a good foundation for mental and emotional health. This is not to say that a person from a happy, normal home will never experience problems and difficulty later on, nor will they always deal with them in the best possible way, but generally they will respond in a healthy, appropriate manner to the problems of daily life. Whereas someone who has spent the first eighteen years in an unhealthy, dysfunctional family may find themselves struggling with a mixture of painful emotions. Our emotional memory stores up all the events that have had an emotional impact upon us. The brain uses a simple but efficient method for making sure emotional events are registered in a marked way. The same chemicals that alert the body to danger also stamp the moment vividly upon our memory. Under stress or anxiety, or intense joy, a nerve running from the brain to the adrenal glands triggers a secretion of hormones which surge through the body preparing it for action, but these same hormones also carry signals back to the amigdala, the emotional memory bank. This stimulus to the amigdala seems to imprint in the memory moments of emotional arousal with added strength.[2]

I remember praying once for a young man who was in a state of severe anxiety. He was facing the life-changing decision as to whether or not he should ask a girl to marry him. On the surface it seemed to be the decision that was causing his worry. But many young men have faced similar challenges and not fallen prey to such an anxiety state. As we probed into his life history, he said he often suffered from anxiety and had done so since he was a small boy. I asked him about his family relationships and at this point he broke down as the memories came tumbling back of a childhood dominated by overly strict parents. He remembered always being anxious because any small error on his part would be punished, often by a beating. He spent his life being afraid to take decisions in case they turned out to be wrong ones.

I recently read the following story of a young man whose ability to relate intimately to women was affected by something that happened to him when he was a small boy.

When I was about five or six, I told my mother one evening about a girl who lived near us and who was in my first grade class at school. I thought I loved her, I said. Some day I would marry her, I predicted, and we would live down the street not far away so that I could come home and have dinner every evening. Kind of dumb, huh? But that's not the end of the story. An evening or two later my mother entertained a group of women in our home. I was in bed trying to go to sleep when I began to hear peals of laughter from downstairs. Wondering what it was all about, I tiptoed to the top of the stairs and began to listen. They were talking about their children, exchanging stories about crazy things kids do and say. Suddenly, I heard my mother begin to tell the women what I'd confided to her a few days before. And what made it worse for me was the realisation that the mother of the girl I'd talked about was there in the group.

I can't describe what it did to me to hear my mother telling my secret to those women, especially to that other mother. And the feeling was compounded when my mother made a joke of it and everyone joined in even greater laughter. It was as if I'd been stripped of everything. And I remember thinking that night, I'll never tell my mother a secret ever again. And I wonder if that was the night I decided I'd never tell any woman my secrets. For the only thing worse than my mother's voice was the pain of that laughter. I feel a coldness in myself whenever I hear women laugh at a table in a restaurant, or in a corner at a cocktail party. I have this irrational feeling that they're cackling about something some man said or did.[3]

Past events need to be thoroughly cleansed and laid to rest if they are not to invade the present. When I was expecting my first baby I was ill with hypertension and had to rest. One afternoon when David was away I haemorrhaged badly and had to be whisked away to hospital by ambulance. I had rarely been ill until that moment, except as a child of three when I had had diphtheria and had been rushed off in similar frightening circumstances. The second event of dramatic and sudden illness completely undermined my confidence. I became anxious, afraid that someone in the family would be taken suddenly ill. Even ten years after the event the mention of hospitals would grip me with fear and I would quickly change the conversation. I wish I had known earlier that there are ways to let God heal our painful memories.

Incorrect Belief System

Closely related to past events are the beliefs or assumptions we have made during the formative years of our childhood. Out of the things that happen to us, the teaching we receive and the modelling we see, our attitudes about life, relationships, love, marriage, God, church, work, play etc. are formed.

> My attitude is my angle of approach, a mode of thinking – a mental posture I adopt when approaching things. Attitudes are like magistrates sitting in judgement on the events of life. They are silent observers who look at and listen to life's circumstances, poised to bring judgement at any said moment. Attitudes are those lenses through which we view things. As a result they affect our perspective on life.[4]

Unfortunately many of our attitudes come out of faulty assumptions and need updating, but in most instances we go on believing them and act them out in our practices.

As we have already seen, the signals we receive from our sensory organs can travel straight to either the feeling part of our brain, or to the thinking brain. When the signals pass through to our thinking brain one would assume the process would then be logical and rational, except that when we have stored up some incorrect assumptions, then we judge every experience in the light of those false or out-of-date beliefs. So beliefs such as: 'This family doesn't wash their dirty laundry in public', may prevent any sharing in depth with friends outside the immediate family. It can result in emotional isolation, unnecessary guilt and burdens being carried which would have been halved if shared. Every time something happens to cause grief, anxiety or fear the signal goes to the brain and gets passed through the misguided grid of: 'This family doesn't share'. Sadly we believe what we believe, even when it's irrational!

I remember chatting with a young girl who grew up in a home where daddy had to be kept happy. He ruled his family with fear. When he was in the house everyone tiptoed around him, afraid of his outbursts if anyone put a foot wrong. No wonder my young friend was such a people-pleaser and extremely concerned about keeping the peace at all costs. She would grow very fearful at any sign of conflict. On hearing raised voices her anxiety would mount. She would put the experience through her mind and tell herself that conflict resulted in pain; someone always got hurt. So her reaction was either to escape or placate the person, sometimes compromising her own values to do so. It meant she was fearful in relationships and unhappy with herself.

Prolonged Stress

Another trigger for our bad feelings may be prolonged stress. When difficult circumstances continue for too long our mental health may be jeopardised. Sometimes the causes are circumstantial. The person may be caught in a trap from which there appears to be no escape. I remember praying once for a lady who had a daughter suffering from anorexia. The child seemed intent on killing herself. The mother, along with the medical profession, seemed impotent to stop her. Month after month the mother struggled with fear and frustration and eventually depression. The stress had lasted so long that she was on the edge of collapse.

The Mental Health organisation, MIND, lists difficult family backgrounds, suppressed feelings, stressful life events, bio-chemistry and genes as possible causes for mental distress. Obviously we will not be dealing with bio-chemistry but sometimes there is an imbalance in our body chemistry which needs some medical help. It is not easy to know what comes first – the chicken or the egg. Has the prolonged stress, for example, caused the body chemistry to go wrong or is it the other way round? No one really knows. But it is worth attacking the problem on both fronts, with drug therapy and counselling.

Our genes may certainly pre-dispose us to certain feelings. Recently a team from Hopkins University and the National Institute for Drug Abuse in America discovered that the reason some people can tolerate pain and others have a very low pain threshold has a genetic base.[5] So if our genes have a bearing on our pain toleration they may also pre-dispose us to certain feelings. A person may be prone to a quick temper, like Dad, or inclined to worry and anxiety, like Mum. However, this doesn't give us permission to indulge our feelings. We still have to learn to deal appropriately with things like anger and anxiety.

Certainly a difficult family life can predispose us to stress. However, this could be halved if only there was a greater support system around families. The breakdown in family life has increased the stress level considerably. 'In the absence of good support systems, external stresses have become so great that even strong families are falling apart.

The hecticness, instability and inconsistency of daily family life are rampant in all segments of our society, including the well-educated and well-to-do.'[6] A very disturbing piece of data came out of a massive survey of parents and teachers which showed a worldwide trend for the present generation of children to be more troubled emotionally than the last; more lonely and depressed, more angry and unruly, more nervous and prone to worry, more impulsive and aggressive.[7] If family life is not restored, the next generation will be even more stressed out than this one.

Stress is on the rise, particularly in the work place. It is one of the main contributors to work absenteeism. The five most common causes of stress, according to an Industrial Society survey, are: life events such as divorce, moving house or marriage (57%), an increased workload due to downsizing (56%), job insecurity (46%), rapid change (41%), and in joint fifth place, long working hours and difficulty balancing home and work (31%).[8] Put the causes relating to work together and the responsible family man or woman is trapped in very difficult circumstances. Add on to that a fear of failure, low self-esteem or a need to prove themselves, and the scene is set for a potential breakdown.

Circumstances, or our misconceptions, may be the cause of our bad feelings, but these are not the only triggers. Something more subtle, less obvious, may be at work within us.

Our Motives and Goals

Motives are driving factors in our lives. They may be out of sight and hidden, even from ourselves, or totally obvious to ourselves and to others. Every child is born with similar basic needs to be loved, to be valued and to feel he or she can achieve. If these are adequately met by caregivers, something within the child is satisfied and the drive to meet these needs does not become a motivating factor in the years ahead. A child who has experienced major rejection will be left with a longing to be accepted, loved and wanted by other people. This could become a driving force in her life. If it is, she will be motivated to set goals which will fulfil those needs in some way. I remember meeting a woman who had made a disastrous marriage. She told me about her unhappy childhood and how she had dreamed of having her own home, with children and a husband who loved her. She ran away from home at a young age and married a man she hoped would fulfil her dream of happiness. But he abused her and eventually left her. Her hunger had blinded her and coloured her judgement.

I once spent some time in the home of a very wealthy man who had been shamed and bullied as a child. His father had deserted the family, leaving them nearly penniless. His mother had scrubbed floors to keep the wolf from the door. He had never had the right equipment for school and the other boys wouldn't let him forget it. He decided early in life that to be valued by others he had to be successful. It became a motivating factor in his life. His particular goal, which he hoped would meet this need for success, was business; it could equally have been sport, theatre or some other activity. He was fortunate because he achieved his goal, but what if he had failed or found his goal to be unreachable? He would have suffered guilt, depression, and perhaps anger if another person had got in the way of his desire. After meeting him I was left with a question in my mind. He had set his heart on riches in order to be a person of value, now that he was rich did he feel of value? He had spent so much time telling me of all his business successes that I had begun to wonder if he still felt like a 'nobody' on the inside, and this was the reason he had to keep underlining what a 'somebody' he was.

We all have a degree of unmet needs within us. We live in a broken world and no one is totally whole. This means we will always feel hurt when our security, self-worth or significance is threatened. Being aware of the needs that tend to motivate us can be a major step forward. The reaction we have to disappointment, criticism or failure will alert us to the deficits in our lives. A number of years ago I was attending a counselling course. One evening we were told that one of us was going to be asked to counsel another person in front of a video camera. The rest of us would be asked to watch and then we would all spend some time discussing the session – or in other words criticising it. To my horror I was picked out to act as the counsellor. My immediate reaction was to refuse. No way was I going to open myself to being criticised by thirty other people. The course leader challenged me. 'Is your value tied up in what other people think about you?' he asked. I knew at once that he had hit the nail on the head. My value was tied up in that very thing. Being a success in other people's eyes mattered to me. In fact I did it and people were kind to me so it wasn't as painful as I had thought it was going to be! But the incident served a good purpose. It alerted me to my need to be valued. Since that time I have worked on my sense of value, so that, though it's not pleasant to be criticised, it is not something that I would lose sleep over any longer.

None of this means that being motivated or setting goals is wrong. Motivated people are energised and envisioned and, provided God is Lord of our motives and our goals, amazing things can be done for the kingdom.

We have already looked at the eight major feelings. The four negative ones were: anger, anxiety, fear and guilt. It is sometimes possible to trace these feelings back to a fairly simple cause. I have often used this rule of thumb myself and found it very useful in trying to understand why I may be feeling, anxious, sad, frustrated etc.

When angry, look for a blocked goal, hope or ambition. When something comes between us and a strong desire or hope we are often angry with whoever or whatever has obstructed our desire. I have a friend who is a perfectionist. She hates untidiness, sloppiness or lateness. However, she works with two people who have a tendency to be all three. Every now and again she will lose her temper with them because they continually block her desire to have a neat and tidy life.

Some of our goals may seem trivial at first sight, but they are nevertheless important to us. We invest time and energy into the things we value and therefore enjoy. When they are threatened or taken away we become angry. A few years ago I spoke to a very distressed lady. She was both angry and sad at the same time. For many years she had run a successful women's Bible study group at her local church. She loved the ladies that attended. Some were elderly and it was their one outing of the week. Much of her time and energy was taken up with this group. Then a new Rector came to the church and after a year decided to close everything down. He felt the church needed to stop their activities and start afresh. He may have been right, but my friend felt he was insensitive and unwise. How could he close something that served a purpose in the community? It was obvious that she was having difficulty knowing what to do with her bad feelings. Her desire to look after those ladies was being blocked and she was angry with the person she felt was responsible for the blockage.

When anxious, look for an uncertain goal. I once had to go to London for a morning meeting. The journey should take less than an hour from Chorleywood, but I like to be punctual so I set off in very good time leaving more than two hours to get there. No sooner had I turned on to the A40 into London than I realised the journey would be a slow one. I tried to tell myself it would not matter if I was a few minutes late. But gradually my anxiety mounted as my goal of being on time became more and more uncertain. The traffic came to a complete standstill halfway into London, and I had to find a phone box and say that I would not be able to get to the meeting, even by 11 am. My goal then became a failed one and I felt guilty and embarrassed.

Sometimes our goals are to do with our family. As parents we long for our children to be happy and safe. But they are individual people and as they grow up they have to make their own choices and lead their own lives. I often receive letters from parents worried and anxious about their children because they are sleeping with their partners, not attending a church etc. Our anxiety will not help the children one iota, whereas our prayers and our trust in God will. Then there is the anxiety we feel when a loved one is sick. Illness always produces anxiety because it brings home the uncertainties of life. Just the other day we heard of the sudden and unexpected death of a young woman with three children. At first the feeling was one of shock and concern for the family, but later the little niggle of worry crept in. This could happen to any of us at any time. None of us want our families to face that sort of pain, but it is impossible to ensure ourselves, or our families, against suffering.

When something we have longed for doesn't happen and we finally realise that we are looking at a failed goal, the feeling will probably be guilt, or shame. I remember arranging one of our early holidays abroad. I studied the maps, looked at the brochures trying to find a place that would suit the four of us who were going. I particularly wanted it to be nice for my husband, who doesn't like holidays at the best of times. When we arrived at our destination I discovered to my horror that our room was dark and pokey, the balcony too small to sit on and it faced a huge unfinished building site. Besides this, the nearest beach was narrow and noisy. All told the holiday, to my mind, seemed doomed to failure and I blamed myself. My dreams of a delightful relaxing holiday in beautiful surroundings lay in ruins. In fact the situation was saved for me, because my husband settled in, got the inspiration for a new book and from then on didn't even look out of the window!

A young man of eighteen confessed to having slept with his girlfriend. He was a keen Christian and had determined to be a virgin when he married. In a moment of temptation and weakness he had failed. His goal could never be achieved. He was for a while distraught, consumed with shame and guilt, not because he didn't believe that God could forgive him, but because he had failed to meet the standard he had set for himself. He knew God could forgive him but could he forgive himself?

Depression or sadness has many causes but could be caused by an unreachable goal.[9] The Bible says that 'Hope deferred makes the heart sick'.[10] An elderly lady I know becomes depressed every now and again. The depression coincides with visits from highly successful friends. Her husband never reached the heights she and many others had anticipated for him. As the years have gone by her hopes for him have slowly diminished and she has realised her goals for him are unreachable. With her realisation came sadness, which is triggered every time she is made aware of other people's success.

The cause of our bad feelings may be the goals we have set our heart upon which have not turned out as we originally hoped. They could also be caused by preconceived ideas, or even wrong assumptions about God and his ways.

Preconceived Ideas about the Fulfilment of Prophecy

When Jesus went to the cross the disciples were filled with fear, disappointment, anxiety and sadness. They had been with Jesus for three years. He had talked intimately with them and told them often what was to come, but it never seemed to sink in. Their preconceived ideas seemed to get in the way of hearing him.

At the beginning of John's Gospel Andrew went to find his brother Simon and said to him, 'We have found the Messiah.' Simon would have envisaged the fulfilment of the prophecies concerning the coming Messiah. A great warrior King to re-instate the kingdom of Israel and save them from their enemies, the Romans. With these thoughts in mind the disciples followed Jesus joyfully, perhaps even hoping that they would get important places in the new kingdom. It was these preconceived ideas that probably prevented them from hearing what Jesus clearly taught for the next three years about what was going to happen to him and what the new kingdom was going to be like.

On one occasion Peter confesses Jesus as the Christ, but as soon as Jesus started teaching how he must suffer many things and be rejected by the elders, chief priests and teachers of the law, and that he must be killed and after three days rise again, Peter took him to one side and began rebuking him. Hearing Jesus talk like that filled Peter with anger and anxiety. Jesus quickly discerned that Peter's mind was still filled with human thinking, which Satan was able to use, instead of a mind open to hearing God's plans and purposes.[11]

Jesus told them many times about his death and his resurrection and yet when the women came back from the empty grave the disciples did not believe them because their words seemed like nonsense.[12] No wonder God tells us that his thoughts are not our thoughts, neither are our ways his ways. Because as the heavens are higher than the earth so are his ways higher than our ways and his thoughts than our thoughts.[13] The distance between our preconceived ideas and goals and God's plans is often greater than it is possible to imagine.

Even after the resurrection and before the Ascension the disciples still had a vestige of their old thinking hanging around. They asked Jesus if at this time he was going to restore the kingdom to Israel.[14] It wasn't until the Holy Spirit of Truth came upon them and blew away their preconceived ideas that they began to comprehend something of the plans of God.

Many a church has suffered the disillusionment of prophetic words apparently not coming to pass. Perhaps someone has prophesied a coming revival and foolishly put a date to it. Disappointment results when the date comes and goes and no revival has happened. Or even more upsetting is the pain of receiving a prophetic word about the recovery of a sick member of the congregation which isn't fulfilled. A friend of ours received such a word about her sick husband. When he eventually died she had not prepared herself for his death, because she was sure he would be healed. She was shocked and angry that God appeared to have let her down. When my husband was in charge of a church he had a ruling that the group who had gathered to pray for a terminally sick person should not give any prophetic words about the person's healing. He felt they were too emotionally involved to be able to hear God clearly. If, however, there was a word from someone completely outside the situation who did not even know the person was sick, then, along with other confirmation it could be worth listening to.

Biblical prophecy and words given by individuals are rarely clear and easy to interpret. When God spoke to Aaron and Miriam about Moses he said to them: 'When a prophet of the LORD is among you, I reveal myself to him in visions, I speak to him in dreams. But this is not true of my servant Moses; he is faithful in all my house. With him I speak face to face, clearly and not in riddles;'[15] Prophecy is like a riddle; difficult to unravel and discern. Paul suggests that it is like seeing a poor reflection in a mirror.[16]

With any prophetic word it is better to do as Mary did with all the words and promises she had received about the baby Jesus. She stored them up in her heart.[17]

Preconceived Ideas about Answers to Prayer

When we pray and nothing seems to happen it is easy to become despondent or frustrated. We easily make the mistake of determining the way and the time our prayers or hopes are to be achieved. I remember a few years ago when the Toronto Blessing was at its height I felt sure we must be on the brink of a full-scale revival. We had prayed for revival for many years and suddenly it seemed that what we hoped for was in sight. I had all sorts of good ideas of how to encourage it, but no one seemed to agree with me. I became angry with those I felt were trying to block what was happening. Then I did the little test. 'Why was I angry?' The answer came back, 'Because your goal is being frustrated.' I argued back, 'But it's a godly goal.' Then I realised I was being presumptuous. I was taking on a prerogative that did not belong to me. The times and seasons are in God's hands. He is the one who decides 'the when' and 'the how' for answering prayer, and for bringing his great purposes to pass.

How easy it is to become impatient with God. We are frustrated because he doesn't appear to be responding, in the way we want, to our urgent and pressing needs. Usually this impatience is caused by our view of God.

A Wrong View of God

One of the major reasons for our bad feelings is our inability to trust God. Paul wrote: 'I have learned to be content whatever the circumstances. I know what it is to be in need, and I know what it is to have plenty. I have learned the secret of being content in any and every situation, whether well fed or hungry, whether living in plenty or in want. I can do everything through him who gives me strength.'[18] How could Paul write that from a prison cell? Because he had learned to trust God. As far as Paul was concerned God was in charge. He was content to let God be God. He knew that 'all things work together for the good of those who love him, who have been called according to his purpose'.[19]

It is difficult to trust God when we have a twisted view of him. Many of us are wearing out-of-focus glasses when we envisage God. For a variety of reasons the God of the Bible is not the one we believe in. We have concocted another God made out of our own ideas. What causes us to hold these incorrect images?

Our Experiences of Fathering.

The experience we had of being fathered will have caused us to make assumptions and hold attitudes about fatherhood in general. It will have affected our relationship to men and authority figures. When we first learned the Lord's prayer: 'Our Father who art in heaven . . .' we probably had a caricature of our own fathers in mind. For me it was always a tired man behind a newspaper. For others it may have been an angry-looking man with a big stick, or a kindly, affectionate, but preoccupied, man who now and again appeared from his study to give them a nod.

Whether we know it or not the way we related to our earthly fathers will have affected us greatly. At a recent conference a young girl came forward wanting God's blessing. I began to pray for her and in the process asked God to show her his love. I prayed aloud: 'Father please show her your love.' The moment I said those words she dropped to her knees and began to cry out, 'I can't receive it. My dad never loved me. How can God love me?'

In a recent edition of the *Soul Survivor* magazine there was a letter from a girl asking the resident Agony Aunt for advice. 'I don't want this to sound stupid,' she wrote, 'but is it wrong to feel you can't ever call God your Father?' Well, it's not wrong, just tragic. Our human fathers were put there by God to protect us, provide for us, encourage us, affirm us and love us. When this doesn't happen we are left with some painful feelings. There may be guilt because of a father we could never please, or fear because of a father who was too strict, or anger because of a man who abused us, or sadness because he was absent and unavailable to us. These are the sort of feelings which are then transferred onto God. We constantly expect to get the same response from God as we did from our own fathers.

Having a distorted view or a limited view of God will inevitably lead to bad feelings every time we face problems, or suffering.

Misunderstanding about Suffering

While Jesus was on this earth he healed the sick who came to him. He cast out demons; raised the dead; stilled the storm; walked on water. His power appeared limitless. Even when they put him on a cross, killed him and buried him in a tomb, he rose from the dead. He appeared to many people, ate with his disciples, and walked through doors in his resurrection body. Jesus is still alive and here with us by the power of his Holy Spirit. Why then do we still suffer? If we believe that Jesus is still able to heal people today and that his miraculous powers are still available to us, then it is easy to fall into the trap of expecting that he will automatically relieve us of our suffering. A misunderstanding of the kingdom which came with Jesus and is yet to come in all its fullness, will lead to these wrong conclusions. The culture we live may also inadvertently accentuate this view.

Cultural Values

Like it or not we are affected, or may be 'infected' by our culture! The society in which live influences us. Many of its values we discard because they are obviously wrong, but others we allow to infiltrate our thinking, without taking the time to weigh them up in the light of Scripture. The television advertisements tell us to buy this or that because 'You're worth it'. In other words you deserve to feel happy, look good, be comfortable. Our society endlessly and relentlessly pursues pleasure and the 'feel-good' factor as if it were our right. The welfare state has educated us to presume that all our needs should be taken care of and if they aren't we feel let down and must find someone to blame or sue. In some churches health, wealth and happiness are actually preached as promised by God. Suffering and sacrifice, two very important themes in the Bible, are understandably not popular. In fact in very many churches they are never mentioned. This sort of wrong thinking inevitably leads to disappointment and disillusionment as the cultural goals for a pain-free, pleasure-filled life are never, or only partially, achieved.

It may be difficult circumstances, past or present, our motives, our misconceptions, particularly those relating to God, or it may be that we have been influenced by the society in which we live; whatever is triggering the difficult emotions we need to deal with them in a biblical and healthy way.

Review

1. What is the trigger for the negative emotions you most often experience?
2. Describe an experience which has recently made you angry, anxious, guilty or depressed. Does this emotion have anything to do with a goal you may have set yourself?
3. Write a description of your earthly father. Does this have any connection with your view of God?

Four

HEALING THE PAST

As we seek to deal appropriately with our difficult feelings we may know, for sure that it is a present circumstance which is triggering our emotional response. We may be dealing with the situation effectively and know that in time the feelings will abate and life will return to normal. But what if the feelings are posing us a real problem. We can never seem to be rid of them. What then?

If it is a present situation bothering you, you first need to consider taking some action. But perhaps that is not possible or you have already done all you can, but are still left with the difficult feelings. It is possible that the feelings are due to some unfinished business from the past which is being triggered by the present situation. There is a difference between the usual irritations, frustrations and sadnesses of everyday life and the unreasonable reaction of a 'hot button' being pressed.

Healing

Many books have been written on emotional healing. I have added to their number! However, it is worth repeating that we cannot by-pass the normal healing process and get away with it. Wounds have to be cleansed and given time to heal. A child, teenager or adult who has experienced a painful loss has to go through the process of grieving that loss before the wound can begin to heal.

Whatever the loss, whether it is to do with our security, value or significance, whether it is great or small, this process is the same. The grief will be of different intensity and duration, according to the person and the cause, but the process is the same. Whether we do our grief work at the time of the loss or years later, it is still the same process we must go through before healing can be achieved.

God placed us in families and I firmly believe he meant our tears to be shed and our wounds healed, within that family. 'The family that feels together, heals together.' However, for many reasons this often does not happen. Parents are too busy, repressed or damaged themselves to give time to drawing out their children and encouraging them to talk about their feelings. Grandma and Grandpa would be only too glad to find the time, but they probably live hundreds of miles away. Children will avoid their pain if there is no one to support them in it. Their little hearts may be breaking but they dare not begin to express their grief for fear it would overwhelm them, which it possibly could. I remember many years ago seeing a lady who was very depressed, and had been for most of her life. As she came into the room to meet us her opening statement was: 'It's my mother's fault.' Throughout the few hours she was with us she repeated the statement several times. Her story was tragic. During the Second World War she was a small child, living in London. One day her mother bundled her into the car and drove her into the country to visit an aunt she had never met before. While her mother and aunt drank tea together the child was sent to play in the back garden. Suddenly she heard the car start up and as she ran to the front of the house she was in time to see her mother disappearing down the road. She began to chase after the car screaming for her mother to return; but the car continued on its way until it finally disappeared back to London without her. The child collapsed on the road sobbing. As she remembered the scene she said to us, 'My mother did it – she drove me mad.' I could visualise that little girl and the excruciating fear that she must have felt. Abandoned – unprepared, in a strange place, with a strange woman. In that moment fear had overwhelmed her; she had felt she was losing her mind. To protect herself from such frightening feelings she must have numbed the pain by suppressing it and instead became depressed. Such grief is too frightening for any child to experience alone.

When the normal, God-given way of emotional healing is by-passed we can suffer a variety of consequences. The only remedy is to go back to square one and begin again. The grief work has to be done sooner or later. Wounds must be cleansed; unfinished business finished. Whether an adult does this alone or with someone else depends upon various factors. Someone working through a present situation of loss can usually grieve with just the support of family and friends, unless of course the present loss triggers some unresolved past issues, or the grief is highjacked by a growing depression. In that case we need someone to talk to. Interestingly a recent survey found that 45 per cent of people put someone to talk to at the top of their list for what they felt they needed when in distress.[1] Many people ask me whether they can deal with past hurts on their own. This may be possible, providing the hurts are fairly minor. Any major trauma should be worked through with another person who can pray and give the necessary support. When a childhood trauma is eventually brought into the light, it can be almost as frightening as when it first happened. The childhood fear of being overwhelmed will return. At a recent conference a lady asked me to pray for her bad back. She was a well-dressed, apparently well-got-together lady, but as soon as I invited the Holy Spirit to come she began to cry. She explained that when she was six her little brother had died and six months later her father had drowned. Her mother was so consumed with grief that she had little energy left for her little girl. The child had just had to swallow her feelings and get on with her life. She had put on a good front, but now the Holy Spirit was penetrating her defences. The grief she began to experience was excruciating. 'I think my heart is breaking,' she said, between her sobs. That sort of grief is too painful to express alone, one's own natural protective defences will prevent it happening. Only in a safe, supportive environment will a person be free to express such a degree of buried pain.

Working Through Loss

When you lose two sons in tragic accidents and another disappears into a gay lifestyle you learn how to grieve. That was Barbara Johnson's painful experience. The process she went through provides helpful guidelines for others. She states that the first response to loss, particularly when it is unexpected, is *shock and unbelief.* 'Oh no, it can't be true,' is the instant reaction. 'Surely I'll soon wake up and find it is all a bad dream.' Even something relatively trivial will call forth this response. Many years ago I had to send my laptop processor back to the manufacturers to be serviced. They accidentally wiped everything off the hard drive; the memory was gone. I was totally shocked and could not believe all my letters, talks and ideas had just disappeared. I remember feeling numb with shock. For about a week I stumbled around just mumbling, 'I can't believe it. How could they have done such a thing?'

Barbara Johnson says that 'Shock is God's way of cushioning those He loves against tragedy. Going into shock gives you time to absorb what has happened so you can try and adjust to the news.'[2] But when the shock wears off the *pain* kicks in. This is when the tears begin. Tears are God's way of cleansing the wound. As the despair, regret, anger, abandonment sweeps over one again and again, the tears begin to flow and slowly the wound is cleansed. Tears are for healing. Several years ago I read an interesting article in *The Times* headed 'Tearful Chemistry'. The writer said that while there may appear to be little apparent difference between tears caused by unhappiness or onions, there is a marked chemical difference. Apparently there had been a First World Congress on Tears and the scientists reported having discovered that tears shed through emotion contain not only water and fatty substances but a chemical named enkaphalin, a naturally-occurring, morphine-like substance which is known to play an important part in controlling emotions and pain.[3] Arthur Janov, promoter of Primal Therapy, states that there is a release of stress hormones in tears. He believes that crying is an important biological function and that shedding tears is central, not incidental to the release of stress.[4] There is no doubt that tears help to diffuse pain. How long this painful stage may last is up to the individual. 'Avoiding grief postpones recovery. Clinging to grief prolongs pain.'[5] The more we can go with the pain the quicker it will pass.

So we are first shocked by painful circumstances, then

engulfed in the pain of the situation, but there may be another reaction we experience at the same time and that is *anger*. Our anger can be indiscriminate. We are angry with the doctor, with the sympathisers, with the other people involved, with ourselves, with our friends. We may even feel angry with God, who allowed it to happen. Certainly it is better to express our anger to God than vent it on other people. God is big enough to take it; they may not be!

It is important that you *drain your pain*. Find a safe way of venting your anger. Pound a pillow rather than your spouse. Throw plastic plates not your best china. You can be certain it will pass and the *recovery* stage will come. When finally all the tears have been spent all that is left is scarring. No one ever forgets painful events, but the memory of the event becomes less and less painful. I was present at a conference when a young man was asked to give his testimony about the way God healed him following sexual abuse by his stepfather. He agreed to share but, as an aside, said that actually he hardly ever thought about it these days, and when he did the pain was no longer there. I had watched that same young man going through the grief process years earlier and as he had sobbed then on someone's shoulder I had wondered if he would ever recover. But washing it away with tears had its healing effect. In fact once the hurt has been healed there is often space inside for some happy memories to surface.

How often I have witnessed adults grieving childhood suffering, and felt incredibly sad for all that they have had stolen from them in terms of joy and happiness, only to be surprised a few weeks later to have them recount a particularly happy memory. Somehow getting rid of the pain had given room for the good memories to surface.

Beware of discouragement when healing is only partially accomplished, or recently finished. It is common to spiral back again. 'Your healing is not a straight line,' writes Henri Nouwen. 'You must expect setbacks and regressions. Don't say to yourself, "All is lost. I have to start all over again." This is not true. What you have gained, you have gained . . . When you return to the road, you return to the place where you left it, not to where you started.'[6]

Wrong Assumptions

Once we have realised that our beliefs are partly to blame for our bad feelings then it is time to take action. Paul encourages the Christians of the first century to have their minds renewed. There is no better advice for the twenty-first century. Jesus said the Holy Spirit would lead us into all truth. We need to open up to the work of the Holy Spirit and specifically ask him to show us where our thinking is not biblical. We should view our lives through the lens of Scripture.

Usually our thinking is renewed gradually as we welcome the Holy Spirit's work, read Scripture regularly and make our lives accountable to those in spiritual authority over us. But occasionally we need to take more drastic action. If we are struggling with difficult feelings it behoves us to take a fresh look at our lives. It is an opportunity to open our hearts before God and pray the prayer King David prayed: 'Search me, O God, and know my heart; test me and know my anxious thoughts. See if there is any offensive way in me, and lead me in the way everlasting.'[7]

Then, if we become aware that some of our false assumptions are to blame for our bad feelings, the next step is to renounce them. It's like repentance. When we become aware of sin we have to confess it and turn from it. The same applies to our irrational beliefs. We have to recognise them as wrong, renounce them and turn from them. But just as wrong behaviour has to be replaced by right behaviour, so wrong beliefs have to be replaced with right ones. I have heard many depressed people say: 'I should never have been born.' If I believed that I would probably feel depressed too, until I recognised it for what it is – a lie! Such people have to work at replacing these thought patterns with something more in line with Scripture. A daily reading of Psalm139 would help the truths contained there to sink in. 'For you created my inmost being; you knit me together in my mother's womb . . . All the days ordained for me were written in your book before one of them came to be.'[8]

'I am such a failure', is another common belief which causes guilt and a sense of hopelessness. How often I have said to such people: 'But that's not true, look at your life. You are not a failure.' But my opinion doesn't seem to change them. Changes begin to happen once they start to believe the word of God. Jesus said to the epileptic boy's father, 'Everything is possible for him who believes.'[9] Paul wrote to the Philippians: 'I can do everything through him who gives me strength.'[10]

As we correct our wrong thinking we sometimes need some healing for the painful beliefs we have held about ourselves. In most cases our thinking is a result of our upbringing. People may have said careless or insensitive things about us, or to us. We may have absorbed the wrong attitudes which prevailed in our home or community. Therefore in correcting our wrong thinking we must not forget to forgive those who have hurt us or contaminated our thinking, and to open our hearts to the healing that only God can give us.

Choice

One of the most important things to realise about any change is that we are responsible for it. We are not robots or puppets. God will not willy-nilly put us on the operating table and open up our minds and place a new set of beliefs in our heads. If we know that our thinking is unhealthy and causing us problems, then we are responsible for renewing our minds. We have to choose to place ourselves under the scrutiny of Scripture and when we read the truth we are responsible for believing it or not. It is a choice. We can continue to believe the lie, or decide to believe the truth and live out our belief by changing our minds and behaviour.

A few years ago I had a conversation with a young man I will never forget. It left a deep impression upon me. This man had had a miserable childhood. He had been placed for adoption at birth, and this had turned out badly. He had never felt wanted by anyone. He was angry and sullen. Despite the fact that a number of people had tried to come alongside him, he said that nothing ever worked. No one could help him. I made one or two suggestions along the lines of healing for his past. His response to me was, 'Been there, done that, got the T-shirt.' I walked sadly away from that conversation wondering what would happen to him. At present, despite what everyone was telling him, he was choosing to stick with an old identity. He knew that Jesus was holding out a new one to him, like a new overcoat, but he couldn't bring himself to dump the old one and take up the new offer. The choice is always ours. It's risky. But that is what faith is made of. Referring again to Victor Frankl's book about his time in the concentration camp, one of his main messages is about 'choice'. He asks the question: 'Do the prisoners' reactions to the singular world of the concentration camp prove that man cannot escape the influences of his surroundings? Does man have no choice of action in the face of such circumstances? . . . The experience of camp life shows that man does have a choice of action.'[11] His conclusion is that man can choose his attitude. He may not be able to change his circumstances but he can choose his attitude in those circumstances. He calls it the last of human freedoms.

Forgiveness

As we gradually work through the painful events past and present, at some point there will most likely be some forgiveness to release or receive. In the course of our lives we get hurt. If we think another person bears some responsibility for that hurt, whether they actually do or not, then a part of the healing process will be to forgive that person. Rationally we may know that he or she could not help what happened. We still need to forgive such people from our hearts. There will be no closure to the wound until this is done. This is not to say we always have to tell them we have forgiven them. It can be between us and God, but for our own sakes it needs to be done. Until we forgive we are bound to the person and it is impossible to break free and move on.

It may be we need to release forgiveness to another or it may be that we need to ask forgiveness from God and perhaps from others. We are always so quick to protect ourselves that we often react to our hurt in ways that hurt other people. A young woman was working through some childhood anger towards her mother who had always been too busy or tired to give her much attention. She had got to the point of forgiving her mother when she suddenly thought about her own reaction to her mother's neglect. She remembered the ways she had punished her mother, and in fact was still punishing her; how she would refuse to share things with her when she knew that she would love to have heard them, or she would be too busy to go out with her. Repentance for her sinful reaction was the final closure to her wound.

Sometimes our reaction to the hurts we have received is to rebel and do things we later regret. Many young people have messed their lives up in this way. Two young women I know became promiscuous as a result of childhood rejection and neglect. In their desire for love and affection they went looking for it in all the wrong places. Though God cannot take away the consequences of our rebellious actions he will forgive us and in an amazing way 'turn the curse into a blessing',[12] when we repent. Both these young women eventually found that Jesus could meet their deepest needs as well as forgive their sins.

Comfort Others
Lastly, for those who have walked the path of healing and have learned how God can comfort and heal, give it away to others. It really seals one's healing to comfort others with the comfort you have received.[13] To walk with another in their pain is a great privilege and something God has prepared for those who have suffered. It is as if you have passed through the university of suffering and come out

with a degree! A friend of mine went through a terrible time of anguish. She had a still-born child and later lost a toddler by drowning. She spent several years grieving her loss, but eventually got through the worst and then for several years ran a still-birth organisation, coming alongside people who were grieving the loss of a child in this way. I am sure her own healing was sealed as she did this.

It is important that unfinished business in our lives is cleared up. We want nothing to cloud our current vision. However, when the past is dealt with the present is still with us and we may still find ourselves struggling to come to terms with some unhappy circumstances. Perhaps we need to look at the possibility of taking some practical action.

Review

1. What past experiences, if any, still cause you pain?
2. How do you think God wants you to deal with them?
3. Is there anyone you still need to forgive?
4. Ask God to show you any irrational beliefs you may still be holding.
5. Write them down and ask God to give you a scriptural replacement.

Five

TAKING ACTION

Painful feelings are rarely caused by one thing only. There are usually a variety of reasons which add up and cause the sense of dis-ease. For example, middle-age can be a crisis time for some men, but usually not for just one reason. The family is at its most expensive stage and there are constant demands on its finances. Work may not be as fulfilling as it once was and the hoped-for promotion is less and less likely to happen. The time spent at work continues to spiral, leaving little time for recreation and exercise. Unwanted weight increases and then there's the odd palpitation of the heart which produces that niggle of anxiety. It may be possible for a man to take action on one or two of these issues, but for the most part only a change of attitude will see him through the crisis.

Before we investigate how a change of attitude can help us, we must first consider how taking some action could alter a situation which is continually provoking an unwanted emotional response. Doing something to alter the situation often seems to be the most obvious way forward to an observer, but some people seem unable to take this apparently simple step. People sometimes ask for prayer to relieve them of their bad feelings, but often when they describe their circumstances it is obviously not so much prayer for the emotional state they need, as prayer for the willingness to make some changes in their lives.

Recently a young wife told her pastor that she thought her husband was having a nervous breakdown. He was very stressed, not sleeping and behaving weirdly. He had always had a nervous temperament, but had been normal and happy until he had been given promotion at work. Now he was continually wound up and seemed very near the edge. It seemed obvious to everyone else that the job was the problem and that he needed to talk to his boss about changing back to the work he enjoyed and could cope with. Sadly it is unlikely that he will want to do this. It is hard for people to make changes in their standard of living. And even harder to lose face with other employees.

Similarly I once talked to a very stressed mother, whose husband had lost his job and was unable to find another. They were in debt and making some very nervous trips to their bank manager. I suggested they might have to cut their cloth to fit their pocket. But the thought of cancelling the riding lessons, the private tuition and moving the children from a private school to the local comprehensive, was out of the question in her mind.

Making some changes might seem the obvious step to an observer, but for a variety of reasons, the changes are often too hard to even contemplate for the person concerned.

An Unrealistic Attitude

When questioned, people will give a variety of answers as to why they are not 'doing something' about a difficult and constantly irksome situation. What often paralyses them is their thinking. Many of us indulge in magical thinking. Somehow we hope the problem will evaporate into thin air, rather like the disappearing woman in the magician's cupboard. 'Abracadabra!' and she's gone! The belief that the problem will just go away by itself is an avoidance of reality. It is one of the attitudes that can eventually lead to a breakdown. Nothing is done, the stress slowly intensifies until at last breaking point is reached. Then something drastic has to be done.

'I shouldn't be feeling like this,' is another thought that prevents action. Shame and fear cause us to suppress our feelings and do nothing about them. We are of the opinion that it is not right for a Christian to experience certain emotions.

'It is not really as bad as all that', is another avoidance game. Everyone around the person can see the stress increasing but taking action seems worse than putting up with the problem. Normally the underlying cause of this unrealistic attitude is fear.

Fear of the Consequences
We often do not take appropriate action because we fear the consequences. We may argue that the time is not right or it is not serious enough yet, but the real reason is that we fear what will happen if we do take action. This sort of anxiety is usually to do with loss. It may be a financial loss, the loss of a relationship or a loss of personal significance or value. Most of us will do all we can to avoid any of these losses. It is very hard to lower our standard of living, even harder to lose friendships upon which we have come to depend. But most of all we hate to feel worthless or a failure in our own eyes, or in the eyes of others.

Change will often be the outcome of taking action. Again few of us welcome change. Thoughts of change can cause anxiety, but for some people change is particularly disturbing for other reasons. Most of us have grown up in homes where our needs for security and self-worth are often inadequately met. Unmet needs cry out to be satisfied. We search for significance in the things we do. We look for security from our relationships and our sense of value is constantly fluctuating, depending upon our performance and other people's opinions. Without a clear sense of who we are in Christ and a knowledge of our value to Almighty God, we are left floundering and fearful. 'People can't live with change if there's not a changeless core inside them. The key to the ability to change is a changeless sense of who you are, what you are about and what you value.'[1] Once the 'changeless core' is established it is possible to look at change without being gripped by anxiety.

A few years ago we observed a friend of ours go through a painful time of healing. Every Sunday she would go forward for prayer and then the Holy Spirit would take her through about half an hour of grief. She didn't share with others what was going on until the one Sunday when she suddenly opened her eyes and said, 'Well that's it. I am off to the mission field.' We were amazed. She had a very responsible job, a nice house and car. Why would she want to leave England at her stage of life? Apparently she had felt called to foreign missions about twenty years previously but had allowed herself to be side-tracked. Some painful things had happened to her, but during those sessions of healing; God had done a wonderful new thing in her life. She came through that experience a changed person. To the observer she seemed to have a new knowledge of who she was and a new security in God. With amazing self-composure she set about the huge upheaval of resigning her post, selling her house, going into training and leaving for Asia. Her 'changeless core' had been established.

Lack of Energy

We may know that action is needed and we may have faced up to the loss and the change the action may involve but perhaps we lack the energy for it. This lethargy usually points to the beginnings of depression. Depression has a variety of causes. There may be roots in an unhappy childhood, inherited characteristics, bio-chemical imbalance, all of which may pre-dispose a person to depression. Circumstances such as broken relationships, too many changes, unemployment or overwork, may be the trigger for a person with a pre-disposition, to slide into a deeply depressive state. Everyone suffers moods of sadness and frustration which may last for a few days, and may affect relationships or work ability but normally these moods pass, our energy returns and with it the ability to think creatively about our problems. But a person with a real depression does not recover after a break and his energy does not return.

Depression often gathers strength gradually, almost unnoticeably. At first the victim may use some magical thinking to cope. 'It will get better after the New Year.' Or, 'I will think about it later.' But in fact they are not facing the reality of the situation and when they finally do they are too depressed to take any action. I was once asked to see a lady in her early fifties. It did not take me long to realise that she was quite depressed. She lacked energy, and spent a lot of time sleeping. She made no effort to get out of the house, make friends or find something interesting to do. Apparently it had started when her children left home.

She had invested all her time and energy in them and from this she got her feelings of value and significance. When it was over her life seemed to lack meaning. There were so many things she could have done with her time, but her depression robbed her of her energy, her initiative, and her imagination. Inertia had taken over. Had she taken some action before the children left home she would have had other activities to fall back on, but now she was too depressed to take the initiative. It took help from a variety of sources, and several years, before she eventually found out who she really was, apart from her children, and began to live a more fulfilling life.

These are some of the reasons why people do not take action to deal with emotionally and physically draining problems. But in the end the major reason is a failure to take responsibility for our lives.

Failure to Take Responsibility

John Powell used to have a notice stuck to his mirror over the sink. 'You are looking at the face of the person who is responsible for your happiness.'[2]

Quite simply, our emotional life is our responsibility. So too are our problems. They belong to us, and to no one else; we are responsible for finding a solution to them. Once we accept this so many of our difficulties can be resolved relatively quickly. This is not to say we cannot involve others in helping us, but the initiative for the solution has to come from us. Failure to take responsibility for our problems is a major cause for the unresolved issues in life. We blame someone else for our predicament, or we expect someone else to rescue us. In either case we are expecting the other person to sort it out. Part of maturity is learning to take responsibility for our lives. This is a discipline fundamental to growth. It may be true that our boss, friend or spouse is to blame for our stress. His or her demands may be inordinate. He or she may be inconsiderate and insensitive, but the problem still remains ours because we are the ones feeling the pressure. Once I own a problem then something within me begins to look for a solution. While I am sitting in blame or waiting for a rescue there is no energy for finding a solution.

We have to learn to approach our problems with the attitude that something can be done. Denial, either through not facing reality or not taking responsibility, creates inactivity, which leads on to hopelessness and despair. It is not wrong to have negative feelings, but it is wrong to do nothing about them. In fact change usually comes about because someone has become dissatisfied with the status quo. At a recent conference I noticed a workshop entitled 'The Spiritual Gift of Dissatisfaction'. Though I did not attend the workshop I was intrigued by the title. 'Unhappiness is a good thing when it comes to change. Discontent is necessary for action.'[3]

I recently heard the story of a farmer who every year lost his chickens by drowning. His land was very near the river and became flooded every winter. Year after year he suffered tremendous loss. Eventually he became desperate enough to do something about it. He changed to duck farming!

In every situation that evokes difficult feelings it is important that we take action. As we have said it may only be possible to change our attitude to the situation. It may not be possible to change the core problem. We may only be able to ease it, or manage it better. But whatever action is appropriate something must be done. Remember, when we do nothing we are actually making a choice. However, when we are in the grip of a negative emotion, choosing to do nothing is not a good choice. If my children have been rude and disobedient, sitting everyone down and confronting the issue would seem better than staying awake all night worrying about it. If fear of a burglary nags me it would be best for me to save up and get a burglar alarm fitted.

Be Pro-active

Being pro-active means more than taking initiative.

> It means that as human beings, we are responsible for our own lives. Our behaviour is a function of our decisions, not our conditions. We can subordinate feelings to values. We have the initiative and the responsibility to make things happen. Look at the word responsibility – 'response-ability' – the ability to choose your response. Highly proactive people recognise that responsibility. They do not blame circumstances, conditions or conditioning for their behaviour. Their behaviour is a product of their own conscious choice, based on values, rather than a product of their conditions, based on feeling.[4]

Being re-active means that we have allowed conditions and situations to control us. We respond out of our feelings instead of our values.

Someone once came to me and reported a conversation she had overheard. The comments included a second-hand report of something I was meant to have said. I was furious and immediately tackled the person whose comment had been overheard. In effect I reacted to third-hand gossip without ascertaining the truth first or even stopping to consider how best to tackle it. The anger and desire for action were understandable but the quick reaction was wrong. It was a mistake and I learned that there are right and wrong ways to take action. My response needed to be a choice based on my values. Values such as the dignity of the individual, unity of the body of Christ, truth, peace and love should have directed my response. If I had stopped to consider these values I would have made a different choice.

A few years ago a friend of ours was found to have a very invasive form of cancer which ultimately would not respond to treatment. Her reaction was to obtain the truth about her illness and then, with a detailed diagnosis and prognosis, to take time to discuss the whole situation with her family. Together they considered the options. She was a Christian woman who believed that death was not the end. She had no desire to leave her family but nor did she want to prolong her life for a few extra months if there was no quality to it. In every way she was pro-active. She took responsibility for her life and death. Her final choice came out of her firm Christian belief in the resurrection from the dead. She chose not to have treatment and as a result died within four months of diagnosis. Her last months were a time for saying goodbye. There was an amazing dignity in the way she chose her attitude to death and it spoke volumes to everyone who witnessed it.

Ask Questions

In our efforts to be pro-active we need to ask questions; primarily of ourselves, and maybe of others, but only if they can help us clarify the situation and not just sympathise with our bad feelings. When trying to resolve issues that involve other people it is best to go straight to the source of the problem – your boss, your friend, your spouse etc. and not to gossip around. Rather than deal with a problem head on we all have the tendency to talk to others hoping perhaps that they might tackle it for us, or at least sympathise with us. 'Going to a third party can invite psychological games.'[5] However, there is a place for seeking advice of a wiser, more mature person who is outside the situation, providing we know that we are honestly not trying to involve this person in some triangular game. Seeking advice may be part of the ground work towards taking action. Abe Wagner who is an international management consultant suggests that you ask the person you are seeking advice from not to tell you what you want to hear, but to give you an objective response, even if it means confronting you about your role in the conflict. In fact he would only occasionally go to another person for advice. He prefers to tackle the problem at source. Abe Wagner tells how his friend Abe Polonsky used to confront him for moaning and groaning about his boss. Polonsky would smile and ask Abe, 'How did he respond when you told him about it?' Wagner would rapidly get the message and go and knock on his boss's door.[6]

However, before going to the source, ask yourself some questions. Only as you become aware of what is going on within you can you be in a position to take action. Stephen Covey, writing about highly-effective people, says that he has worked with many different people: business executives, college students, church and civic groups, families and marriage partners – all people who deeply want to achieve happiness and success. But he says that he has never seen any enduring solutions to problems, lasting happiness and success, that came from the outside in.[7] Solutions come from the inside out. We start resolving our problems first within ourselves by asking important questions such as: 'What am I feeling? Is it fear, anger, guilt, loss, jealousy, anxiety?' Then, 'Why am I feeling like this?' Having ascertained the answers to these questions you are in a position to consider what you can do about them. The next step is to check out the possibilities.

Go Through the Possibilities

In considering the correct action it is important not to make a hurried decision. 'All things are created twice.'[8] Visualise your action first. In fact visualise each of your options and find the one that you think will be the most effective. Then you need to go through your action step by step. A few weeks ago we had someone coming to see us with whom we had some difficult issues to sort out. It was important that what we said was understood clearly, so we sat down and talked it through together, discussing how it would be best to put it across, looking at all the various options. We even decided who should say what. The next day we approached the interview with more confidence and clarity and for the person concerned this was very helpful.

Next rehearse the possible consequences in your mind. As you do this you are preparing yourself for any changes. As you consider the possibilities one of them could be to seek for clarification.

Seek Clarification

Clarification is a better word than confrontation. For example, if an employee is consistently late for work it would be better to ask him to come and see you in order to clarify some issues than simply to confront him. There may be a good reason for his lateness and there may be a need to adjust his timetable. Or he may have just got slack and needs reminding. Of course it may be the other way round and you are an employee being asked to do more than was in your job specification. In such a case, asking for a meeting to clarify some issues with your boss would be a good place to start.

It is easy to become upset by listening to rumours. All second-hand information needs confirming before any action is taken. A friend of ours who is the pastor of a large church was told that a member of his staff had behaved improperly with a young girl in the congregation. Although the pastor was very angry and disappointed, instead of confronting the young man immediately he set about clarifying and checking the information thoroughly first. Eventually he was convinced that the information was correct. His next step was to see the young man; he told him that he needed to clarify some issues with him and tackled him about his behaviour with the opposite sex. In fact the man admitted to conducting himself unwisely and agreed that for the time being he should step back from ministry while he received some counselling. Nothing is ever lost by taking one's time clarifying all the issues. In fact it will result in a wiser decision.

Ask for What You Want

'One of the most efficient ways of getting what you want

is to ask for it.'[9] This does not necessarily mean you will always get what you want! But until you ask you will never know. We may often assume that because people are not doing certain things that they do not want to do them. People are not mind-readers and we wrongly assume that everyone will know what we want without us ever telling them. If you are feeling resentful because the family never give you a hand with the housework, try asking for their help. Perhaps they haven't noticed your tiredness. Maybe you have always done it and the family have come to take you for granted. But a simple request might produce the desired results.

My husband has a tendency to be untidy and spill out of his office into the kitchen. After a few weeks of watching my worktop getting smaller and smaller I begin to feel irritated. This is my signal for action. My first step is usually a request for his co-operation and usually he looks surprised – as if he hadn't noticed the clutter! Then he gathers the stuff together and dumps it in his study, where it belonged in the first place. Occasionally he nods in agreement but does nothing, so then I have to resort to my next tactic, which is to gather it up myself and dump it in his office!

When we perceive that our bad feelings are caused by other people's behaviour, one of the temptations is to try and change that person by nagging. It is an unattractive and bad habit which is easy to fall into when we are continually frustrated by someone. The problem is that nagging rarely changes another in the way we want it to. Constant moaning, criticism, and 'put-downs' usually cause the recipient to shut off or dig their toes in stubbornly. They may even punish the nagger in subtle ways which exacerbates the situation rather than resolves it.

If we ever find ourselves in this type of situation, either of nagging or of being nagged, something must be done about it. Continuing the dysfunctional behaviour will not help the situation one iota. The nagger needs to apologise for resorting to such unhelpful behaviour and then be open about what he or she wants. The nagged person needs to say how it makes them feel, and also why they are finding it difficult to change. Perhaps it may be possible to come to a compromise. It may be that they are trying to work together and assuming that they both want the same things, but in fact their aspirations are very different. This is often the cause of friction in a marriage situation. I realised at a young age how different a husband and wife's goals may be. My mother was a very strong, motivated woman with a lot of energy. Her own childhood had caused her to value material security and she was very motivated to achieve this. My father was an unambitious, quiet man who just wanted a peaceful life. Their goals clashed and was the cause of constant bickering in the home.

It takes courage to sit down with one's close friends or relatives and find a way through these sort of situations. But we have a choice, to continue in a deteriorating relationship or to take some appropriate action. In expressing how we feel we need to remember that self-control is a fruit of the Spirit. Providing we are able to control the expression of our feelings it's good to say how a situation has made us feel. For example, if someone is rude or insensitive in his or her dealings with you, there is a place for saying how the behaviour has made you feel. But if you know that you have a tendency to become very emotional, and such a show of emotions would be inappropriate, then it would be a better choice to shelve dealing with it until you have had time to cool down.

Change an Agreement Which isn't Working

Flexibility is an important attribute in any situation. Sometimes we make agreements with other people and later discover that there are weaknesses and we need to make some adjustments. For example, say you have agreed to look after a friend's pre-school child every Tuesday morning. This is fine until your husband begins to work at home on a Tuesday and needs the house to be quiet. As you struggle to keep a lively toddler quiet, you find yourself becoming resentful both of your friend and your husband. The agreement you have is no longer working out, so there is only one way through and that is to change it.

Young couples today usually start married life with both of them working full-time. In the beginning they probably make some agreement about the household chores. After a few months it may be obvious that the agreement is not working very efficiently. Rather than continue until both partners are totally frustrated and fed up, it would be better to sit down and make a new agreement, which, after the months of trial and error with the old one, is likely to be more realistic.

When we lead conferences in other countries we send our timetable ahead, knowing from experience the best order and length for sessions. Sometimes, however, it doesn't work as we planned and we are forced to change the programme. It may have worked well in every other country, but customs differ from place to place and if they don't fit with our timetable it is better to change the order than be irritated by people not turning up at the right time.

Similarly when we lived in Chile we quickly learned the word '*manana*'. Chileans never seemed to be in a hurry and to them people are more important than punctuality. We often had regional conferences on a Saturday. The timetable would be made out, the speakers for morning and afternoon arranged. At first we were disappointed and frustrated because it rarely went as planned. It was a case of learning to be flexible or have a breakdown. In fact the missionaries who didn't stay were usually those who couldn't adapt to the more relaxed atmosphere of South America.

Change My Behaviour

In the process of taking responsibility for a problem and for finding a solution we sometimes realise that we cannot change the situation, nor can we change the other people involved. The only element we can change is ourselves.

When I was at boarding school we were forced to eat large boiled onions in a white sauce. I have loathed onions ever since! When I got married I knew very little about cooking, but one thing I did know and that was that I would not be using onions in anything! However, after a few months of eating tasteless cottage pie and stews, and living with a disappointed and frustrated husband I had to change my behaviour. I cried as I sliced the onions! But there was only one resolution to our problem in this case and that was me changing.

Recently, a young woman complained to my husband that she kept losing jobs. She was uptight and angry with those who had sacked her. Unfortunately her work brought her into close contact with people and her problem was her unfriendly attitude. So my husband suggested she had two options. One was to change her career, the other was to change her manner. As her career had involved many years of training it seemed more sensible to get some help to improve her 'bed-side' manner.

Establish Priorities

At each stage of life priorities change. What is important to you at thirty may not be top of your list at sixty. As you look for a way through the present difficulties ask yourself the question: 'What do I want?' A couple I know had lived in a lovely house for many years. They had a large circle of friends and a good church, but the children had all left home and the house and garden were too big. They were beginning to feel depressed and worried about the upkeep of the property. Eventually they sat down and listed their priorities. They wanted a small house and garden within walking distance of the shops. Those things took top place on their list. Then came the family, friends and church. They decided the family wouldn't mind travelling a slightly longer distance to visit and that they were still able to make new friends and join another church. But the all-important thing was to make a move while they were still young enough to cope with these changes.

It is easy to feel that our needs and what we want are priorities. A woman who has been at home looking after the children all day probably thinks that sitting down with her husband when he comes in from the office and sharing what sort of day she has had to be quite important. She can feel very resentful when he goes glassy-eyed, or he keeps glancing at the television while she is in the middle of describing the baby's latest trick. A talk to oneself about priorities would probably deal with the resentment. Food first for a tired husband, then the news and then a chat about the day's events would probably work best.

Change Your Circumstances

Listing your priorities may, as in the example of the elderly couple, mean a change of circumstance. As one gets older drastic life changes are not undertaken lightly. But now and again they are the only action left to us. A friend of mine lost her husband. Then her children became independent and, at about the same time, her mother became rather infirm. My friend was constantly worried about her mother and wished she lived nearer; she didn't enjoy driving and hated the long journey to see her. She was torn because she had lived in her present house all the time the children were growing up and she had many friends in the neighbourhood, but her anxiety nagged away. Eventually she decided that the problem would not be resolved by doing nothing, so she sold her house and moved to be near her mother.

Recently a lady told me that her husband had been unfaithful to her several times in their marriage. She was angry and felt betrayed. The first time it had happened she had forgiven him and taken him back. The second time she did the same. But now, she told me, it looked as if it was happening again and she did not know how she was going to cope with her bad feelings. About a year later I heard that she had left him. Apparently she had confronted him about his behaviour, but he could not promise that he could control his 'weakness'. By staying with him she felt she would be condoning his behaviour and so she moved out and into a flat.

At times couples have complained to us that their church has nothing to offer their children. They have several choices. They can sit in a church that is unlikely to change and become frustrated and anxious as they watch their children becoming more and more bored and disillusioned. They can start something for children themselves, or they can decide to move to a church where there is something better going for children and young people.

Perhaps at this point it is worth mentioning the importance of keeping a godly attitude when an unhelpful church situation impels us to leave. King David gave us an exemplary model for leaving a destructive situation. Saul set out to kill him so David was forced to leave the king's court and go on the run. He left alone although he could have done what Absalom did many years later, when he incited a crowd of his father's subjects against him and went to Hebron where he was made king. But David left alone. Later he was joined by others – mainly bandits. Even then, when presented with the opportunity to kill Saul, who after all was trying to kill him, David refused to harm the Lord's anointed leader. David, we are told, was a man after God's own heart. It is hard to leave a church situation without taking others with you, and even harder not to speak badly of someone who may have been a poor leader, made mistakes and caused a lot of pain. But in the end God honours those who have a right attitude.

Occasionally, the best action would be to physically move away from a difficult situation when it seems to be unchanging. But say, for some reason, that option is out of the question. Perhaps our children are at a crucial stage in their education, or our job is in that particular locality. We may have aged parents to look after, or the difficult situation involves a responsibility that we cannot walk away from. One choice then remains. We have to find a way of emotionally handling the situation. Clearly something within us has to change.

Review
1. Is there a situation in your life that needs some action?
2. What is holding you back?
3. Which of the options for action would be the most appropriate?

Six

CHANGE OUR GOALS

The purpose of this book is to find ways of handling negative and often unwelcome feelings, so that our lives may have a healthy stability. Perhaps taking action is not an option open to us. In that case we may need to look at a change of attitude. As I have previously suggested one of the main triggers for these difficult emotions are the goals we set for ourselves. We all live with aspirations and longings, of which we may or may not be conscious. When these are not achieved, as hoped, we can easily become disillusioned and disappointed.

To Recap:
Blocked Goal   = Anger, frustration
Uncertain Goal   = Anxiety, fear
Unreachable Goal = Sadness, despair, hopelessness
Failed Goal   = Guilt, shame

If we think this may be our problem what can we do about it? First we need to take a good look at our goals, asking ourselves what our hopes and longings are and what has caused us to have these aspirations?

Motives
'Motives propel us to action. The word "motive" is derived from the same word as "motion" or "motor". Just as a

motor drives a vehicle, so motives are the propelling force behind the way we act and the direction we take.'[1] Or, 'A motive is a thought pattern with feelings, and values which lead to energised behaviour . . . Motives lead you to action – the action has a goal.'[2] It is, in fact, the energy which keeps us striving to achieve certain ends.

We are motivated people from the beginning of our lives here on earth. At first the baby is motivated to get his needs for food and warmth met. Later, food may not be top of the list. As a toddler he may be more motivated towards people who meet his needs for security and pleasure. Our youngest grandson is two years old and is highly motivated to receive all his father's attention. If his older brother dares to sit on his father's lap his goal is to oust him and take his place immediately. If this is blocked then he becomes angry, and tries harder. When this doesn't work he doesn't lose his motivation. In fact it becomes stronger, so he changes his tactics. He usually agrees to share the lap for a while, but gradually it becomes obvious that he is taking up more and more of the space and eventually his older brother becomes tired of the struggle and gives up. It is fascinating to watch this same struggle in adults. It may not be for daddy's attention but to be noticed by a person in authority. I remember once being at a conference which my husband was leading. Two young men were keen to capture his attention. Though they were both gifted, they were unsure of themselves. It was interesting to watch them vie for his attention, and then to see one of them finally give way to the other.

Our basic motives do not change much. Our need for security, approval, achievement, significance and a sense of value, tend to motivate us throughout our lives. People who have failed to have these particular needs satisfied in childhood, are often highly motivated towards getting them met in adult life. In the broken world we live in, where children are hurt, let down and deprived, despite all the parents' good intentions, it is impossible to have these needs fulfilled in the complete way we would have all liked. So we are left with hunger in our hearts which motivates us towards gaining satisfaction.

Our needs are not the only things which drive us to set goals. Other things have a part to play. Our siblings, our extended family, teachers and friends all play their part in our lives. As we interact with them we have thoughts and feelings from which we mentally underline the things we value, then out of those values come our priorities. We start to place certain things above other things. For example in our relationship with our siblings we may consistently win the games and as we do so it feels good. The feeling that success brings us is enough for us to set that as a priority. Another influence is the culture we live in. As we grow up in a particular geographical area, with a certain type of people, at a certain time in history, we are affected negatively or positively by what we experience in that culture. Out of our feelings and thoughts about the experience we form certain values. A strong influence on my own life was the books I read as a child and teenager. They all seemed to have a high moral tone. They encouraged one to reach for qualities which were very idealistic and slightly unreal, but on reflection I think I prefer them to some of the violent literature read by children today which elevate power and control as good values.

We are not always aware of our motives. 'All a man's ways seem innocent to him, but motives are weighed by the LORD.'[3] If we are ever to change our goals then we need to understand what it is that motivates us.

Self-awareness

'The purposes of a man's heart are deep waters, but a man of understanding draws them out.'[4]

As we have already seen, in some situations our 'emotional mind' responds more quickly than does our 'rational mind'. Often what happens next is the 'rational mind' immediately stamps on the feelings as if they were out of order, wrong or stupid, and then proceeds to rationalise about the situation. However, it is important that the two responses work together to bring emotional intelligence to the situation. The feelings could provide us with some important information.

We should seek to become men and women of understanding. Knowing what is in our own hearts is a good safety-net and only when we know this can we set about making changes. In our search for self-awareness we should start by making inquiries. 'Everything depends on the quality of your questions and the truthfulness of your answers.'[5] When we are struggling with negative emotions a good place to start would be to ask ourselves why we are feeling, for example, depressed, angry, fearful or anxious. What has been said or what has happened to make us feel that way? It is a simple question which is not always easy to answer. Frequently people tell me they are in the grip of a painful feeling and have no idea why. King David prayed: 'Why are you downcast, O my soul? Why so disturbed within me?'[6] In another psalm he prayed that God would search him. 'Search me O God, and know my heart; test me and know my anxious thoughts.' Sometimes we have to open up our lives to the scrutiny of the Holy Spirit. On one occasion a young girl asked for prayer because she kept feeling unreasonably fearful. She had no idea why this feeling kept gripping her heart. As she opened herself to the Holy Spirit she began to remember little snippets of her childhood. She saw herself cowering away while her father shouted at the family. She had not remembered this part of her childhood because when she was still a child her father had become a Christian and had changed into a much more patient and loving man. Previously he had been rather a controlling bully. She had been a timid, nervous child and had been afraid of his angry outbursts. With these memories came the understanding of why she had always wanted peace at all costs. This desire was a driving force in her life. Unfortunately she could not control those around her and often things at work would become quite tense and the noise volume would increase. Then she would feel the anxiety level rise within her. It is only as we gain some understanding that we will become emotionally competent. It is the key to handling disputes and resolving conflict.

Impure Motives

Our actions are clear for all to see, but the driving force behind these actions is hidden from view. Scripture endorses this. 'He [the Lord] will bring to light what is hidden in darkness and will expose the motives of men's hearts.'[7] Not only are they hidden but they are clearly not always pure. 'For the appeal we make does not spring from error or impure motives.'[8] This suggests that, though Paul wasn't, others were preaching from wrong motives. Not only can our preaching be from impure motives but our prayers also. 'When you ask, you do not receive, because you ask with wrong motives, that you may spend what you get on your pleasures.'[9]

Because of our fallenness, brokenness and tendency towards independence from God, even Christians can have impure motives. This is what God accused his people of through Jeremiah: 'They have forsaken me, the spring of living water, and have dug their own cisterns, broken cisterns that cannot hold water.'[10] Their sins were first forsaking God and then trying to find their own ways of meeting their needs. Needs cry out for satisfaction, so we set ourselves goals that, if achieved, we think will satisfy our need for love, praise, approval, identity etc. The motives are often impure for the simple reason that they are biased towards self-centredness and towards satisfying ourselves.

Goals

Our goals are not necessarily indications of our motives. On the surface our goals may not appear sinful or wrong. They may be perfectly normal, even altruistic. But we get the red light telling us something is wrong when what we have hoped for doesn't happen and we spiral into negative feelings. Then we should start asking the pertinent questions. 'Why am I angry?' Back comes the answer, 'Because my promotion was blocked.' The next question: 'Why is this so difficult for me to come to terms with? What is motivating my need for promotion?' Of course it may be the simple need for more money with which to clothe and feed a growing family. But then the reaction would be one of disappointment. However, if the need was for significance then the blocked promotion could possibly cause anger. Wanting significance cannot be labelled a wrong goal, yet as Christians we have higher aspirations. Stephen Covey says that, 'The enemy of the "best" is often the "good".'[11]

Temporary Goals

Kingdom goals are ones that have eternal significance. It is very easy to get snared into the world's obsession with wealth and success. A recent programme on ITV, *Who wants to be a millionaire* has had some of the highest ratings both in the UK and the USA. All the contestants have plans for the million they hope to win. Mostly the plans are for short-term pleasure. There is nothing wrong with wanting a new car, a new house or a holiday, but unless they are held lightly they have the potential for disappointment, because they are transient, fallible aspirations with no eternal significance. Sometimes we can miss the best by grasping at some present and passing satisfaction. Many years ago when we lived in South America another missionary was visiting our home. She had quietly and unobtrusively given us a gift. No one was meant to have guessed it was from her, but one of us found out and began to thank her. Instead of looking pleased she looked rather crestfallen. 'Oh dear, now I've lost my reward,' she said. Our eldest daughter was about eight years old and was intrigued by the missionary's response. 'What do you mean?' she asked her. 'Well,' said the missionary, 'you can do your good deeds before men and receive your reward there and then from them. Or you can do them in secret and be rewarded by God when you get to heaven.' Our daughter looked stricken, even angry. 'Why has no one ever told me that before?' she cried. 'Think of all the rewards I've wasted!'

Shadowlands was the title given to a book and a film about the life of C.S. Lewis. I imagine the idea behind the title was that this life, with all its pain and suffering, is just a shadow in comparison to eternity. We often set our hearts on a shadow and wonder why we feel so upset when it turns out to be just that – a shadow.

Failed Goals

None of us enjoy failure. It is painful and often feels like a disaster. But God can use failure for our good. In our western culture many people get on a sort of conveyor belt and have no opportunity to stop and think or take stock. If their pathway is suddenly blocked and they are faced with a brick wall they are forced to pause and consider their lives. Failure to achieve our goals can be an opportunity for God to change the direction of our lives and to redress a wrong balance in our lives. Maybe to uncover some hidden agenda we were not aware was there.

I have told this story many times, but it is an experience which God used to show me something in my life I did not know was there. Some years ago my colleague, Prue Bedwell, and I went to the USA to do a conference. We had a long and very tiring trip over and arrived at about seven in the evening their time, but early morning our time. We were exhausted and not too happy to be kept waiting well over an hour for our hosts to arrive. Eventually they turned up and we settled into the car for another two-hour journey to our final destination. On the journey our hosts explained that they had had some problems in their organisation and they had failed to advertise the conference sufficiently, hence there were only thirteen people registered. They were sorry because they realised that they should have cancelled it and saved us the journey. I remember feeling speechless with anger and Prue had to step in and keep up some semblance of polite conversation. We arrived at our lodging only to discover our room wasn't ready. So we waited in the hall. Eventually we climbed the stairs to bed. By then it was morning our time and we had lost a night's sleep. Exhausted, I closed my eyes at last and as I was about to drop off to sleep a phrase I had once heard came into my mind. 'God offends the mind to reveal the heart.' I went to sleep admitting to God that I was well and truly offended. The next day I spent waiting on God and asking him to show me my heart. As far as I was concerned I was a failure and so was the conference. And yet was it such a failure? What was wrong with coming all this way for thirteen people? Wasn't one person just as important to God as one hundred. Gradually God began to reveal my heart to me. I was angry because other people's inefficiency had caused me to feel a failure. Somewhere over the years I had become ensnared by the 'success' culture. Success is frequently measured by numbers. Therefore small numbers must equal failure. Gradually I realised that my goals had changed. Without me even noticing I had began to aim for success and a feeling that I should be treated differently from the One I served. A blocked goal had caused me to stop and reconsider my values. It was a salutary lesson I shall never forget.

God can use failure to great advantage. Moses longed to rescue his people from their slavery in Egypt. Then he went about his desire all the wrong way and ended up killing an Egyptian. He had to flee from Pharaoh and escape into the desert. He became a shepherd for forty years in the wilderness. How often during those long years must he have regretted his hasty action. After growing up in Pharaoh's court with all its luxury, shepherding must have felt like failure. But God used the experience to humble Moses. In fact years later he was noted for his great humility. 'Now Moses was a very humble man, more humble than anyone else on the face of the earth.'[13] This was probably the reason why God was able to use him in such an incredible way to rescue his people and to become one of the greatest leaders of all time.

Joseph was another. When he was sold to Ishmaelite merchants by his brothers and carried to slavery in Egypt he must have regretted his youthful boasting to his brothers which caused them to be so jealous. Didn't a sense of failure haunt him as he lay in that Egyptian gaol? But God used it. When his brothers finally came down to Egypt to buy corn, though a great man by then, Joseph was far wiser and humbler than before. He understood the purposes of God and that, although his brothers had intended to harm him, God had intended it for good.[14]

God will often allow failure to come into our lives because unconsciously we have set our hearts on temporary or perhaps self-centred goals. The desire to be popular, to succeed, to become a great leader, to gain a reputation or to be comfortable, and God wants to reveal our hearts to us and to change the direction of our lives. 'Feeling good isn't the final goal of mankind, even though many people, even many Christians, arrange their lives around that belief. Rather we are called to glorify God and derive our well-being through him.'[15]

Kingdom Goals

'The things that matter most must not be at the mercy of the things that matter least'(Goethe). What mattered most to Jesus was his Father's will. Even though he was 100 per cent God he was also 100 per cent human and in his humanness he had the potential to have settled for an easier life. In fact Satan's temptations were all about deflecting Jesus from achieving God's will, God's way. But from the beginning God's will was of prime importance to Jesus. St Luke tells the story of Jesus as a boy of twelve. Jesus had been up to Jerusalem with his parents and when his parents started on their way home they were unaware of the fact that Jesus has stayed behind in the temple courts. Eventually they noticed his absence and began looking for him amongst the crowd they were travelling with. When they didn't find him they went back to Jerusalem and found him in the temple sitting among the teachers, listening to them and asking them questions. His parents were understandably cross and asked him why he had treated them in such a way. Jesus responded: 'How is it that ye sought me? Wist ye not that I must be about my Father's business' (KJV).[16]

Several times during his three-year ministry Jesus reiterates this sentiment. 'I tell you the truth, the Son can do nothing by himself; he can do only what he sees his Father doing, because whatever the Father does the Son also does.'[17] 'For I have come down from heaven not to do my will but to do the will of him who sent me.'[18] Then the night he was arrested he prayed on the Mount of Olives: 'Father, if you are willing take this cup from me; yet not my will, but yours be done.'[19] Early in his relationship with his disciples Jesus taught them to pray a similar prayer:

'Our Father in heaven, hallowed be your name, your kingdom come, your will be done on earth as it is in heaven.'[20]

Mother Theresa was once attending a gathering with many important people from all over the world. They were all dressed up in their crowns, jewels and silks and Mother Theresa wore her sari held in place with a safety pin. One of the guests spoke to her of her work with the poor of Calcutta. He asked her if she didn't become discouraged because she saw so little success in her ministry. Mother Theresa answered, 'No, I do not become discouraged. You see, God has not called me to a ministry of success. He has called me to a ministry of mercy.'[21]

Josh McDowell tells the story of a 'head-hunter' whose job it was to hire corporation executives for other firms. When he was interviewing a potential executive he would disarm him and then lean over, look him squarely in the eye and ask him a question, 'What's your purpose in life?' He said it was amazing how top executives would fall apart at that question. Then one day he was interviewing a young man and he asked him the same question. 'What's your purpose in life, Bob?' And, without hesitation, the young man replied, 'To go to heaven and take as many people with me as I can.' For the first time in his career the head-hunter said he was speechless.[22]

There is something very wholesome and selfless about kingdom goals because they come out of a pure heart. J.B. Phillips translates 'Blessed are the pure in heart' as 'Happy are the utterly sincere'. The word 'sincere' comes from the Latin meaning 'without wax'. It was the notice placed on the slabs of marble for sale in the marketplace. It advertised marble whose cracks were not disguised by rubbing wax into them. A second meaning could be 'an undivided heart' or more literally, 'a heart without folds'. 'How often are our good deeds done with mixed motives, a sense of reservation, bias or prejudice? . . . Singleness or sincerity of heart means "to be open, without ulterior motive, unambiguous (having double meaning), whole-hearted, free from pretence." '23

I wonder how many apparently good deeds we do from mixed motives – from a desire to be admired by others, wanting to be loved, to be appreciated, to gain something, either material or emotional from others? A friend of mine has a very rich aunt and she told me how tempting it was to start trying to curry favour so that the old lady would leave her some of her money. 'But I'd be such a hypocrite,' she said.

Maintaining Integrity

As we seek to keep our eyes fixed on kingdom goals which come out of pure motives we have to guard our integrity, by re-examining our heart at intervals and being accountable to others.

Richard Dortch was known as a man of integrity. He became president of the PTL Club (Praise The Lord) to work alongside the successful and popular TV evangelists, Tammy and Jimmy Bakker. Dortch was caught up in the infamous scandal which shook the Christian world in which Jimmy Bakker was found to have committed adultery with a woman, who then accused him of rape. Dortch helped to cover the scandal. Not only that but he went along with Jimmy Bakker's extravagant ideas for a Disneyesque-type holiday complex for which they had to raise millions of dollars. Although Dortch was not purposefully dishonest he nevertheless compromised his integrity by keeping quiet, and went to prison for fraud and conspiracy. At one stage as he pondered his time at PTL he asked himself: 'How had my judgement suddenly become so clouded? Why did the options always appear so complex? Why couldn't I just do what I knew to be right? Why wasn't I listening to my heart? Somehow I realised my integrity was slowly eroding, but I felt powerless to flee from the slippery slope.'[24] After prison, Richard Dortch wrote a book entitled: *Integrity – How I lost it and my journey back.* In it he writes:

> Integrity involves everything about the wholeness of our inner person, our heart, mind and will. Integrity simply means singleness: singleness of our purpose, singleness of our will, singleness of our hearts. There is no dividing of the truth that splits the wholeness of what we are about. It is said that adversity tests our ability to survive, and prosperity tests our integrity. That's when the problem usually occurs, in the times when we are high and above it all.[25]

Success poses its own peculiar temptations, one of which is to become slowly diverted so that one's goals change and the focus of our lives is no longer God's kingdom, but achievement, applause, and comfort.

Kingdom Goals Never Fail

A few years ago one of our sons-in-law lost his job. Naturally I began to pray earnestly for him. I prayed that he would find a new job soon, that he and his family would have enough money to live on and that they would not have to suffer too many disappointments or hardships. Time went by and my praying became more and more anxious. In fact the more I prayed the more anxious I became. Then I stopped and asked myself some questions. 'Why am I so anxious? And why are my prayers making me more so?' Very quickly I remembered what Jesus said in that famous sermon, 'Seek first his kingdom . . .'[26] What would that mean? How could I pray for my family in such a way that would prioritise God's kingdom in their lives? I began to experiment. I started to pray that God would teach them new things through this experience, that they would learn to trust him more through it, and that it would be a refining process. Suddenly I knew I had hit the jackpot. My anxiety began to disappear and excitement took its place. These were kingdom prayers. Prayers that I knew God would delight to answer.

I am highly motivated towards a tidy, organised lifestyle. A style which gives me feelings of security and self-worth. It means I am not very spontaneous or flexible. But I live with a husband who is easy-going, relaxed and definitely spontaneous. This means that my days are sprinkled with interruptions. Only the other day I found myself feeling disappointed because due to my husband's 'good ideas' I had not even begun to achieve the goals I had set for myself that day. Then I remembered someone once said that our interruptions are often God's appointments. With this thought my goals for that day changed. Instead of looking for that secure feeling of being in control of my time, my goal was over ridden with a kingdom one – God's purposes for that day.

So kingdom goals never fail, because they are in the will of God for our lives and those we love. When Barbara

Johnson's two sons were killed and a third became a homosexual she was distraught. But she clung to the Proverb that says, 'And you can also be very sure God will rescue the children of the godly'.[27] She never gave up hope for her gay son. She said, 'I'm here to tell you not to give up hope, particularly when you're in a hopeless situation, because God only gives out the score on a life when the game is over — the game isn't over YET with my kid.'[28] After six years of not hearing from Larry he turned up and asked his parents to forgive him for the eleven years of pain he had caused them. There had been a real restoration to God in his life and now he wanted to be restored to them as well![29]

When Jesus encouraged his disciples to 'seek first' his kingdom he added an interesting addition: '. . . and all these things will be given to you as well'. The things he was referring to were material needs. He was saying that if we will only stop pursuing temporary and transient objectives, and instead make God's kingdom our priority, our other needs will be looked after in the process. Victor Frankl admonished his students not to aim at success —

> The more you aim at it and make it a target, the more you are going to miss it. For success, like happiness, cannot be pursued; it must ensue, and it only does so as the unintended side-effect of one's personal dedication to a cause greater than oneself, or as the by-product of one's surrender to a person other than oneself. Happiness must happen, and the same holds for success: you have to let it happen, not by caring about it. I want you to listen to what your conscience commands you to do, and go

on to carry it out to the best of your knowledge. Then you will live to see that in the long run – in the long run, I say! – success will follow you precisely because you had forgotten to think of it.[30]

Changing Our Goals

'If the ladder is leaning against the wrong wall, every step we take just gets us to the wrong place faster.'[31] If you realise that you are aiming at the wrong thing then change the target. We only have one life to live. How short-sighted we are when we chase after that which will bring us only temporary happiness and end up with nothing of eternal significance to show for our life on earth. On the death of a mutual friend one man asked another, 'How much did he leave?' The friend responded, 'He left it all.'

A Paradigm Shift

Sometimes we need a revelation which will open our eyes to the previously unseen aspects of life. We can all tend to tunnel vision and we need something to stop us in our tracks and cause us to take a deeper and longer look. Some may have such an experience when they are diagnosed with a terminal illness, or they lose a job, or a child is taken ill, and they are suddenly forced to face up to the true values and priorities of life.

What is important, about the picture opposite, is to realise that when we first see it we observe only one thing, either an old hag or a pretty young girl. Then as we study it more closely we are gradually able to see the other picture. What was hidden is now clear. Until someone else presents another point of view we have a tendency to see life through our own personal spectacles – and that can be

very limiting.

I was first confronted with this picture when John Wimber of the Vineyard Fellowship visited St Andrew's Church in 1981. He showed it to start us thinking about changing the way we viewed certain things. Then he challenged us with what was a novel approach to ministry. He suggested that we follow the example of Jesus who found out what the Father was doing, and did that, instead of taking our plans to God and asking him to bless them. Maybe we had always known this, but that day it came to us with great clarity. Another shift was the way we viewed the ministry of healing. We had a seen it in the hands of the priests or superstars, but John showed us that it belonged to the whole body of Christ. He used to say: 'Everybody gets to play.' Carol Wimber recounts an incident at a conference where there were a group of academics who were frantically writing notes. John stopped and said, 'You don't get it do you?' Looking down, he saw some children and called them up to him. There was a crippled man there and John said to the children, 'You pray for him!' 'Pray for him?' they said. 'What do we say?' John answered: 'Just ask Jesus to do what you think needs to be done.' So the little boys said, 'Jesus, heal this man's broken legs!' The man was healed right then and there!

With that single event God taught the academics something that would have taken them years to understand with all their wisdom and scholarship. The ministry of the Holy Spirit is for everyone, man, woman and child.[32]

When we have had a paradigm shift we have to put our new values into practice. Old habits die hard and it will take effort to set our sights on new goals and then keep our lives motoring in that direction.

Discipline

Once while conducting a leadership seminar, John Maxwell defined discipline as the choice of achieving what you really want by doing things you don't really want to do. After successfully doing this for some time, discipline becomes the choice of achieving what you really want by doing things you now want to do! He believes that we can become disciplined and enjoy it – after years of practising it.[33]

I have discovered that nothing really worth while is achieved without discipline. If we want to be healthy it takes thought and exertion. If we want to grow into maturity it takes time and determination to stick with the process. If we want to extend the kingdom it will take courage, determination and discipline. The world, the flesh and the devil are lined up against us. We will be tempted to take short-cuts and detours, especially when the going gets tough.

Keep Going Even When it's Tough

As we seek first the kingdom of God it is well to remember that it will not be an easy option, at least not in the short-term. In the short-term it was a painful, cruel option for Jesus. But in the long-term his decision to go with the will of God caused the downfall of Satan, saved us from our sins and opened the door of heaven so that all who believed could go in and enjoy eternity with God for ever.

When we left England for South America in 1959 I remember crying as we pulled out of Liverpool Docks. It was a grey, drizzly October day, yet England had never looked so beautiful! Five weeks later when we searched for fleas in a cheap hotel near the docks in Valparaiso, I longed for my parents' spotlessly clean home. When I left my baby's dirty bibs in the bathroom, ready for washing, and found that they had been eaten by rats, I was shocked. When the 1960 earthquake devastated Southern Chile I shook so hard my teeth ached. We went to Chile obeying the will of God. In the short-term it was the worst experience of our lives, but in the long-term God changed us through it, and we would not have missed the experience for anything.

There were many times during our seventeen years on the mission field that we had to grit our teeth and keep going. As we seek first the kingdom of God and make that our target in life, there will be times when the going is tough and we need to persevere.

Last year while on holiday in Greece we went for a long walk up into the hills surrounding the village where we were staying. It turned out to be a much harder climb and longer walk than we had ever anticipated. We stopped for a cup of coffee at a wayside inn halfway back, and then began our last lap home. The break had not helped. As I began to walk again my legs felt like lead, but I kept my eyes on David who was a little ahead of me. He kept a good pace and I followed. When it became really hard I imagined the shower and cool drink back at our hotel. Focusing on David and the reward at the end kept me going. When the going gets tough we need to remind ourselves of Jesus and what he endured for us and to keep in mind the eternal values of the kingdom that we have made our goal.

William Barclay has said that endurance is not just the ability to bear a hard thing, but to turn it into glory. Recently I read a little book about an extraordinary woman called Sister Sesharatnamma, or Amma. She had borne terrible suffering in her life but endured, and at eighty she is still travelling the world preaching the good news. Amma became a Christian when she was delivered of evil spirits and healed of a tumour. Her husband also became a Christian but later fell away. She continued to follow Christ even though she was disowned by her family and continually beaten by her husband. At times she was knocked unconscious. The beatings were so severe that many of her bones were fractured. In spite of these difficulties Amma continued to rejoice in the Lord. She made it a goal to fast and pray until the repentance of her husband. She also placed certain conditions before God at that time. God had told her clearly that she was to go to all the places she was invited and spread the good news of his kingdom. For her the conditions she set were like short-term goals which would enable her to fulfil the longer-term goal: Her husband should be converted; God should teach her how to read the Bible (she was illiterate) and how to preach the word of God; her own people should be converted and they should serve the Lord.

Eventually all three conditions were fulfilled and then she agreed to go where ever she was invited to serve the Lord for his glory. She has done this faithfully for many years, during which time she has lost six children, had many threats on her life, spent long weeks fasting, once for three months with only a daily jug of water, eating nothing. At the end of the book she writes:

> It is true that, if we want to follow Jesus, we need to deny ourselves. We need to be ready to meet any kind of danger or persecution for Christ's sake . . . No doubt we face difficulties and problems. Many times we fail. But failures are the stepping-stones to success. So we need to press on, looking forward to the goal. Every Christian (saved) is a runner in the race whose goal is the blessed hope that is the glorious heaven. Only if we run our race faithfully, we can receive the crown of eternal life.[34]

Review

1. What are your personal goals in life?
2. What is the motivating force behind these goals?
3. Think about a difficult situation that you are presently praying about. Is there a different way you could pray which would be more in line with kingdom values.

Seven

A KINGDOM PERSPECTIVE

Sorting out our motives and goals is important in dealing with negative emotions. Learning to live with a kingdom perspective is another invaluable tool. There is no doubt that our world-view affects the way we face the trials and tribulations of life.

'The mystery of the Kingdom is the key to understanding the New Testament and the Christian life,' writes Derek Morphew.[1] It is also a great help in dealing with the painful emotions that arise when we go through times of hardship and heartache. Some of the most difficult issues in the Bible become illuminated in the light of teaching on the kingdom.

When John Wimber worked at Fuller Theological Seminary he met missionaries for the first time who had a completely different mind-set from himself.

Listening to these missionary professors, as well as students from Third World countries, certainly had its effect on John's world-view. He heard their dramatic stories of healings and miracles, as at the same time he was being exposed to George Eldon Ladd's teaching on the Kingdom of God. The already, and the not-yet. The invasion of the Kingdom of God into this present evil age.[2]

When I first heard John Wimber teach on this subject it was for me a paradigm shift. I suddenly had a perspective on many problems that before I couldn't begin to grapple with. Since then, Derek Morphew's book, *Breakthrough*, has unravelled even more of the mystery of the kingdom for me. I greatly value the understanding I have gained from these two men and their writings.

New Testament view of the kingdom can be summarised in four statements: the kingdom will come; the kingdom has come; the kingdom is coming immediately and the kingdom will be delayed.[3] The fact that these statements seem paradoxical is precisely where the mystery lies. How can an event be both future and present?

Jesus thought in terms of two ages – the present and the future. He taught about the coming kingdom and the end of the age (Mt 21–25). But he also taught that the kingdom had already come. 'But if I drive out demons by the Spirit of God, then the kingdom of God has come upon you.'[4] All through his ministry Jesus drove out demons and healed the sick, demonstrating the kingdom's presence. Yet Jesus also taught that the kingdom had not yet come but was coming soon. 'From that time Jesus began to preach, "Repent for the kingdom of heaven is near." '[5] He instructed his disciples to do the same. 'As you go preach this message; "The kingdom of heaven is near," Heal the sick, raise the dead, cleanse those that have leprosy, drive out demons.'[6] As if this were not enough he also taught that the kingdom would be delayed. He indicated this in the parable of the ten virgins. Five of them were foolish because they did not have enough oil to last. The bridegroom was a long time in coming and when he did eventually come the five foolish virgins were unprepared.[7]

These apparent contradictions are the reason why so many have given up trying to understand the end times and the kingdom of God. In fact it is only as we hold these seeming contradictions in tension that we can begin to unravel the mystery of the kingdom.

The Kingdom Has Come, but is Not Yet.

The following illustration originated with Oscar Cullmann. It is a modern-day parable of the kingdom which has come, but is not yet.

During the Second World War the D-Day landings in France proved decisive. Once the Allies had landed in Europe victory was assured. Everyone knew that the war was over – the battle was won. Yet it took months before Hitler finally surrendered and Victory in Europe was declared (VE day). The time between was a period of delay when the final outcome was recognised, but the ultimate victory had yet to come. When Jesus came the kingdom broke through, victory over the enemy was assured and Satan knew it. But just as there was a delay between D-Day and VE day, there is a delay between the victory on the cross, and the final Day of Judgement. That will be the end. The kingdom came with Jesus (D-Day), but it will come in its finality and fullness when he returns on Judgement Day.

The Kingdom is Imminent

Every time the gospel is preached and signs and wonders follow, the kingdom becomes evident – the future kingdom breaks through into this present age. So in that sense it is very immediate. It is just here, and at any moment it could break through and thrill us with its power or amaze us with its grace and glory. On the last night of the New Wine '99 conference in the West of England, the kingdom of God broke through in an extraordinary way. One felt as if anything could happen. There were many touches of God's Spirit with demonstrations of power in healing and deliverance. The fullness of the kingdom felt imminent at that moment. 'When someone experiences the gift of the Holy Spirit, he partakes of the powers of the coming age. Whenever someone is healed, a kingdom event has taken place, and the age to come has broken through.'[8] When you taste of the coming age in this way, it becomes awesomely and obviously near.

The Kingdom is Delayed

In his teaching about the kingdom Jesus also indicated a delay. The gospel has to be preached to all nations to give people opportunity to repent.[9] Until that time the coming of the kingdom will be delayed. During the waiting period people will continue to sin, to suffer and to die. Just as in the delay between D Day and VE day many soldiers were lost. In fact there were more casualties during that time than in all the rest of the war. If God were to take away all suffering and sin now, it would mean that the kingdom had already come in its fullness and power. But God is purposely delaying the event to give more people time to repent.

As I thought about this delay an imaginary, allegorical picture came to my mind. It was of a cataclysmic disaster in which a great chasm opened up in the earth and swallowed all the people. They found themselves caught on ledges and parapets, dangling over a seemingly bottomless abyss. A massive rescue operation was immediately put into action by the 'powers that be'. A huge basket was lowered to where the people were stuck. Some gladly got on board, grateful for the rescue, but others were reluctant. They said that they were enjoying the freedom of the ledges. They could move around from one ledge to another. They liked the view and the company was good. Why should they get into the basket and have their activities curtailed. Meanwhile the aftershocks from the original calamity continued to take place. On occasions the earth shook and many people were killed. Gale force winds created panic among the 'ledge' population and some would leap into the basket to be rescued. But others mocked the 'basket people' and said they didn't need rescuing, they were going to climb to the top on their own. The population in the basket grew daily and they longed for the moment when they would finally be lifted to safety. Now and again messengers from the 'top' would be lowered with provisions and gifts, and the 'basket people' would enjoy a foretaste of what it would be like at the 'top' when that final rescue took place. They longed for the day to come. But the 'powers that be' knew that the basket was the only hope of salvation for the people, so in their passion to see more saved they delayed lifting the basket. Meanwhile the aftershocks were becoming more frequent and violent. The 'ledge' people quarrelled among themselves, some starved because others took all the food, while the 'basket people' were in the middle of it all. On the one hand they were rescued, but on the other they were not yet totally rescued. They were caught in a 'delay of compassion'.

So it is with the church. It is caught in the 'delay' between the times, in a unique dimension where the fallenness of this world and the hope and glory of the future kingdom co-exist.

Healing

When the kingdom finally comes in all its fullness and glory there will be no more sickness, death, pain or crying.[10] God will reign supreme and the devil will be cast down into the lake of fire. Meanwhile we still have sickness in the world. When Jesus came, God's future kingdom broke into the present and many experienced a taste of the kingdom that is still to come in fullness and glory. They were dramatically healed, delivered of evil spirits and powerful miracles occurred. Today when a person is healed it is still a demonstration of the power of the future kingdom. Every healing is a kingdom breakthrough – a sign of the kingdom's power and presence. Even though some are dramatic, for others their miraculous healing is a process. I once watched a young athlete receiving prayer for a damaged knee. The person praying hadn't begun to pray but had just laid one hand on the man. As she did so a slight tremor went through the man's body and in that instant he was healed. At other times a healing happens gradually. A lady once visited a church to ask for prayer for her daughter who had multiple sclerosis. She herself walked with a stick because of painful arthritis, so she was also prayed for briefly. She left the church as she had come in. During the week, however, she found she no longer needed the stick and by the end of the week she had ceased to take the pain killers; the arthritis had greatly improved. She came back to the church the next week to give thanks to God and tell the pastor what had happened.

Why are some healed and some not healed? This is

because the kingdom has broken through but has not yet taken over. It is here but not fully. At the second coming the kingdom will be here for ever. When a person is touched or healed supernaturally by God, at that moment he experiences the future kingdom – it has broken into his present world. The powers of the end of the age have been experienced. When someone we have prayed for is not healed and dies, we are tempted to think God has let us down. Every church which has entered into a healing ministry eventually has to face this problem. Sooner or later one of their most loved members will die of a terminal illness before his time. Members are tempted to give up and not continue with a healing ministry. We should remind ourselves that healings are just tokens, signs of what will one day come in its totality. They give us a foretaste of the end of the age when everyone will be healed and there will be no more sickness. The best is yet to come.

The following story came to me through the internet. It is about a lady who knew she had only a short time to live.

There was a woman who had been diagnosed with a terminal illness and had been given three months to live. So as she was getting her things 'in order', she contacted her pastor and had him come to her house to discuss certain aspects of her final wishes. She told him which songs she wanted sung at the service, what scriptures she would like read, and what outfit she wanted to be buried in. The woman also requested to be buried with her favourite Bible.

Everything was in order and the pastor was preparing to leave when the woman suddenly remembered something very important to her.

'There's one more thing,' she said excitedly.

'What's that?' came the pastor's reply.

'This is very important,' the woman continued. 'I want to be buried with a fork in my right
hand.'

The pastor stood looking at the woman, not
knowing quite what to say.

'That surprises you, doesn't it?' the woman
asked.

'Well, to be honest, I'm puzzled by the
request,' said the pastor.

The woman explained. 'In all my years of
attending church socials and potluck dinners, I
always remember that when the dishes of the main
course were being cleared, someone would
inevitably lean over and say, "Keep your fork." It
was my favourite part because I knew that something better was coming . . . like velvety chocolate
cake or deep-dish apple pie. Something wonderful,
and with substance! So, I just want people to see me
there in that casket with a fork in my hand and I
want them to wonder, "What's with the fork?"
Then I want you to tell them: "Keep your fork . . .
the best is yet to come." '

This awareness of eternity certainly affects the way we
live our lives and the way we face death. On one occasion
John Wimber was flying to Atlanta through a bad hurri-
cane. The plane was being tossed around and everyone was
panicking. The man next to John was downing one whisky
after another and staring at John with unbelief, who con-

tinued scribbling his notes. 'My God, man! Don't you realise what's going on here?' he screamed. Calmly John replied, 'You don't understand. If this plane crashes, I don't have any problem at all. I'm going to heaven. But if we land and I don't have my notes done, I've got a real problem.' He continued writing while they made a messy but successful landing.[11] Wimber had got a kingdom perspective!

One day the kingdom will come in all its fullness and glory. Until that time we have to continue to pray for healing. Every now and again we will see a kingdom breakthrough; even if we don't always witness this, we will still keep on praying. My husband says: 'If you don't do it you will never see it, but if you keep doing it your batting average will go up.'

Suffering

The problems of evil and suffering are the two most profound problems of life, and their enigma has confounded many of the deepest thinkers. Many ordinary people, like us, find suffering a stumbling block to faith. If God is an all-powerful loving God how can he allow so much suffering?

Catherine Marshall, the author, lost her first husband when he was still quite young, and later two grandchildren. She experienced the most intense misery she had ever known at that time. Life went grey. She found the problem of evil and suffering a great hurdle to overcome, until she eventually came to the point of being able to accept that God had allowed it and to ask, 'Lord, what is Your will for me in the midst of these circumstances?' She found new light shed on some of Jesus' best known teachings:

'Are not two sparrows sold for a penny? Yet not one of them shall fall to the ground apart from the will of your Father. And even the very hairs of your head are all numbered. So don't be afraid; you are worth more than many sparrows.'[12]

She was told that the Greek word for 'apart from' or 'without' was a strong word implying more than sympathy or even empathy. The word could be used not only as 'without the knowledge or consent of' but also as 'without the Father's participating presence'. Gradually she was able to accept that nothing can happen to us without his knowledge, his consent and his participating presence.[13]

We may still have a struggle with the concept of God's permissive will, but even this is made easier when seen in the context of a glorious future kingdom. One day this fallen world will end and a perfect new era will be ushered in when there will be no more sin and no more suffering, no more sorrow and no more tears. However, one of the problems about suffering is that when you are in the middle of pain it is hard to think clearly. John Powell suggests that suffering can be so deafening and distracting that it magnetises all our attention and leaves us no peaceful or prayerful place. What we need is a 'previous mind-set', an attitude cultivated consciously in our pain-free moments of peace that will help us in our times of suffering.[14]

Developing a 'Previous Mind-Set'

A helpful fact to remember is that suffering is biblical. The first mention we have of suffering in the Bible is in Genesis when God tells Adam and Eve the consequences of their disobedience. To Eve he says: 'I will greatly increase your pains in childbearing; with pain you will give birth to children. Your desire will be for your husband and he will rule over you.' To Adam God declared: 'Cursed is the ground because of you; through painful toil you will eat of it all the days of your life. It will produce thorns and thistles for you and you will eat the plants of the field. By the sweat of your brow you will eat your food until you return to the ground, since from it you were taken; for dust you are and to dust you will return.'[15]

The outworking of this story in Genesis is that we now live in a fallen world where suffering is endemic. The world is in a bad state. Our greed and carelessness have brought about changes in the climate, damage to the ozone layer, pollution to the land, sea and air. All of which God created for our blessing and enjoyment. We are all sinners and have a responsibility to bear for the corrupt and polluted state of the world. This is not to say that suffering is a direct result of our own personal sin, though it may be on occasions. Suffering is the result of humanity's sin.

Once sin entered the world a process of decay was initiated, and as citizens of the world we share in that decay. The good news is that a limit has been set; there will be an end to it. We have an eternity with Jesus to look forward to. Recently one of our grandsons lost his paternal grandfather. Our daughter had explained to the children that granddad was very ill and would soon be going to heaven, where he would be out of pain and well again. The day after he died our six-year-old grandson came down to breakfast singing cheerfully and telling the rest of the family that he was very happy. 'I am happy because granddad is dead,' he said. They were all slightly shocked; it seemed a little inappropriate when the rest of the family were grieving their loss. 'Why does that make you happy?' asked my daughter. 'Because Granddad has gone to heaven,' the little boy replied. It may have been rather insensitive, but maintaining an eternal perspective is important when we are suffering or facing loss. It can give us the courage to face the problems of life and death.

Sin is part of our problem and so too is Satan. God has allowed him to be active here on earth. Sometimes we have been in danger of becoming dualistic in our thinking and we have given Satan more credit than he merits. God is God and Satan is not God. He is only a fallen archangel whose days are numbered. However, he is active, and within God's permissive will, can still create havoc. But Jesus while on earth continually showed his greater power over Satan. He refused his temptations, cast out evil spirits and took authority over the elements. But it must have seemed to Satan that he had finally won a victory when he put Jesus on the cross; he had misunderstood the purposes of God. Satan purposed it for evil, but God had already planned it for good. 'We know that in all things God works for the good of those who love him.'[16] In fact we can trust that in every single thing, even our suffering, God is working things out for our good, according to his will. '. . . according to the plan of him who works out everything in conformity with the purpose of his will . . .'[17] In the midst of pain we may not be able to see the purposes of God, but we can safely trust that they are there.

It is impossible to read through the Gospels and escape the implication that suffering is part of the discipleship package – suffering is a training school. It was for Jesus and it is for us. Jesus challenged his followers that if anyone would come after him he should 'deny himself and take up his cross and follow me'.[18] Carrying a cross signified that someone was going to their death. Everyone would have known what Jesus was implying.

Our problem is that the media tells us in general that we all have a right to be happy and prosperous. To a large extent even the Christian world has bought into this mind-set, and then we are knocked off track when the reality of suffering hits us. It is normal and human to question God in the middle of a painful situation. Especially when tragedy hits us out of the blue, we can be completely stunned, and the question of 'why' is almost bound to be on our lips. However, we need to recall our 'previous mind-set' – the biblical principles which will act as ballast and help right our listing ship.

As we develop a 'previous mind-set' we also need to take into consideration the fact that suffering can be ben-eficial. So often I have heard the opinion that suffering is such a waste. We can feel robbed by it. But it depends on our attitude whether or not suffering becomes productive or remains meaningless. We often view suffering negative-ly, but in the economy of God it can have positive conse-quences, which in kingdom terms may be highly valued. Going through hardship does more to develop strength of character than when everything is going well. Paul rejoiced in his sufferings because of the perseverance and character that it produces.[19] James encouraged his readers to: 'Consider it pure joy, whenever you face trials of many kinds, because you know that the testing of your faith develops perseverance. Perseverance must finish its work so that you may be mature and complete, not lacking any-thing.'[20] Even Jesus learned obedience through the things he suffered and was made perfect through his sufferings.[21]

When Bishop Handley Moules' teenage daughter was dying of TB, she wrote in her diary that she did not want to waste this suffering – a very mature insight in a teenager!

Difficulties can also have the effect of strengthening our faith. There was once a man who found a cocoon. It began to move about imperceptibly at first, then more energetically. The struggle became so intense that the man thought the butterfly would die from the effort, unless it received some help. So he took a knife and carefully cut the butterfly free. It seemed to enjoy its freedom but it didn't fly away. Concerned, he phoned a friend who taught high school science. As he was explaining what he had done the teacher interrupted him. 'Oh that's the reason. You see the struggle is what gives the butterfly the strength to fly.' It's the same with us. It's the struggles of life, not the easy times, which strengthen our faith the most.[22]

Another benefit is that in the dark times we can experience God's presence and strength in a way we don't when the sun is shining. Paul longed that God would remove his 'thorn in the flesh', which he described as a messenger of Satan. He prayed three times, but God responded, 'My grace is sufficient for you, for my power is made perfect in weakness.'[23] This response completely altered Paul's attitude. Once baffled by them now he boasted about his weaknesses. Recently when I was due to speak at a large gathering I woke in the morning with a very bad headache. I was desperate and wondered whether I would manage it. Friends prayed for me and I cried out to God, but he did not remove the pain. I got up to speak feeling at my weakest. God did some wonderful things that day and though I didn't enjoy the feeling of weakness, I recognised that the dependence I was forced into was the best place to be. But I wished I could stay in that place without having to suffer a thorn in the flesh!

Another benefit of suffering is that it often sets us to one side. Our lives are so full that we have little time to listen to God. One of the consequences of the hard times is that they put us in a better position to hear him. In fact God sometimes permits us to go through hardship because he longs to talk to us but we are too busy to listen. Hosea says that God will allure Israel and lead her into the desert; not to punish her for her unfaithfulness (as she deserved), but so that that he can speak tenderly to her. He even turns the valley of trouble into a door of hope.[24] We have to remember that in the bad times God still loves us and if we will call out to him he can turn the suffering around to our benefit.

It is easy to become weary and discouraged when life is difficult. It may be a help to remember that Jesus suffered profoundly and therefore is able to sympathise with us in our times of trial. 'He was despised and rejected by men, a man of sorrows, and familiar with suffering.' He has been there before us. In fact God purposed it to be that way. 'Yet it was the Lord's will to crush him and cause him to suffer.'[25] So when he comes alongside us and speaks tenderly to us, he understands. This can change our whole attitude – we have something vital to appreciate and something valuable to share with others. 'Praise be to the God and Father of our Lord Jesus Christ, the Father of compassion and the God of all comfort, who comforts us in all our troubles, so that we can comfort those in any trouble with the comfort we ourselves have received from God.'[26]

Many years ago when I was just a young, untried,

curate's wife a woman came to see me with a tragic marriage problem. I remember being speechless. Suddenly all the theory I had learned at Bible College seemed useless. I longed to have words of comfort which came from the experience of having proved God in difficult circumstances. I hadn't long to wait for that experience, but at that moment I had nothing to offer except my time.

Paul had to cope with a tremendous amount of hardship. Imprisonments, hunger, beatings and cold were commonplace in his life but he remained certain that no suffering could separate him from God's love. He challenges us with a question.

> Who shall separate us from the love of Christ? Shall trouble or hardship or persecution or famine or nakedness or danger or sword? . . . No, in all these things we are more than conquerors through him who loved us. For I am convinced that neither death nor life, neither angels nor demons, neither the present nor the future, nor any powers, neither height nor depth, nor anything else in all creation, will be able to separate us from the love of God that is in Christ Jesus our Lord.[27]

Bearing in mind all these things will help us to maintain our equilibrium in the face of heartache and suffering – particularly viewing it in the context of the future kingdom. If we consider this life only it seems like a cruel joke. Paul considered his present sufferings were not worth comparing with the glory that will one day be revealed. The only way Jesus could have borne the weight of what he went through was because he knew what lay ahead. 'Let us fix our eyes on Jesus, the author and perfecter of our faith, who for the joy set before him, endured the cross, scorning its shame and sat down at the right hand of the throne of God.'[29] The best is yet to come!

Jesus had a kingdom perspective, as did Paul after him. This was certainly the key in their lives. However, Paul's letters give us some important insight into how he applied it, and how it helped him weather the storms which constantly buffeted him. From him and others we receive some insights which, if put into practice, will revolutionise the way we deal with problems.

Review

1. Describe a time of suffering. What was your reaction to it?
2. In what way would having a kingdom perspective help you deal with your present-day problems?

Eight

A Two-Dimensional Life

As we attempt to deal with our negative feelings we have a variety of options. We can seek healing if the feelings are being triggered by past events. We can take action, or we can change our goals and live our lives with a kingdom perspective. But even when we have decided to 'seek the kingdom of God' in the middle of a difficult situation it is still easier said than done. Looking at the lives of godly stalwarts who have trodden the path of suffering before us, may provide us some important clues as how to survive the heartaches, and see the blessing of God in the middle of them.

Be Real

'There is a time for everything, and a season for every activity under heaven . . . a time to weep and a time to laugh, a time to mourn and a time to dance.'[1]

There is a time to cry, so when we find ourselves in the grip of a negative emotion one of the first things to do is to acknowledge the reality of how we are feeling. Of course we have to exercise self-control and take responsibility for the how, when and where this should be done, but accepting reality is vital for maintaining integrity. In some Christian circles there is a sickening triumphalism practised, which doesn't ring true and is a denial of our humanity. Mostly it is the result of church members picking up from their leaders what is expected of them. For others it is a fear that owning their true feelings may be dishonouring to Christ. 'Some Christians make the mistake of thinking that grief isn't a "good testimony". They are on the ceiling, climbing the wall, or prostrate before the Lord in their grief, but they feel guilty about it.'[2] Surely God could not have made a mistake when he made us feeling people!

> One of the wonders of the Christian faith in time of suffering is its humanness. Where Muslims resign themselves, Buddhists and Hindus withdraw, stoics endure and existentialists fight in vain, the Christian can exult. But the fierce joy of Christian exultation is not triumphalism. Nor is it superficial. We exult because in knowing God we know the outcome, but this is no protection from the pain of suffering in between.[3]

A brief look at men and women of the Bible should convince us that expressing our feelings is in no way dishonouring to God – it's just being human, the way God made us.

Jesus himself, our supreme example, was not ashamed of his feelings. He wept openly over Jerusalem. He was angry with the money-changers in the temple. He expressed his sorrow to Peter and the two sons of Zebedee when he took them with him to the Garden of Gethsemane. He said to them, 'My soul is overwhelmed with sorrow to the point of death.' He wasn't ashamed to ask them to stay and watch with him and expressed disappointment when they fell asleep.[4] He went through extreme stress when he struggled in prayer that night. The description of his sweat, as drops of blood, indicated this. Jesus was fully human and never denied his humanity for the sake of looking and sounding more spiritual.

Joseph was estranged from his family and in a foreign land for many years. When his brothers came down to Egypt to buy grain and Joseph recognised them, and eventually made himself known to them, he wept so loudly that the Egyptian servants in another room heard him. Even Pharaoh's household heard about it. David was a great warrior but he mourned and wept openly when his friend Jonathan and Jonathan's father Saul were slain. He ordered that the men of Judah be taught a lament in which he publicly expressed his love for Jonathan and his grief at his death. 'How the mighty have fallen in battle! Jonathan lies slain on your heights. I grieve for you, Jonathan my brother; you were very dear to me. Your love for me was wonderful, more wonderful than that of women.'[5] During his reign as king, David frequently expressed his feelings to God in psalms. For example: 'My soul is in anguish. How long, O LORD, how long?'[6] Or: 'How long, O LORD? Will you forget me for ever? How long will you hide your face from me? How long must I wrestle with my thoughts and every day have sorrow in my heart?'[7] And there are many more like these.

Paul, the great missionary apostle, who withstood enormous hardship, was never triumphalistic, except about Jesus. He was real about his sufferings and when it was appropriate, he told others about them. In his letter to the Corinthians he was forced to authenticate his ministry among them for their sake and the gospel's. They were in danger of being deceived by false apostles, so Paul didn't do what one would have expected him to do – boast about all his exploits. No, instead he boasted about his sufferings. 'We put no stumbling-block in anyone's path, so that our ministry will not be discredited. Rather, as servants of God we commend ourselves in every way; in great endurance; in troubles, hardships, and distresses; in beatings, imprisonments and riots; in hard work, sleepless nights and hunger . . .'[8]

Paul listed his troubles and by the time we get to 'hunger' we feel bowed down. A single bad night or one missed meal is enough to depress most of us. But just as the weight of his problems is about to overwhelm his readers, the tone suddenly changes. Maybe he intentionally constructed his letter this way so that the reader's attention would be caught by the change. '. . . through glory and dishonour, bad report and good report; genuine, yet regarded as impostors; known, yet regarded as unknown; dying, and yet we live on; beaten, and yet not killed; sorrowful, yet always rejoicing; poor, yet making many rich; having nothing, and yet possessing everything.'[9]

Live a Two-Dimensional Life

These verses make Paul sound as if he was suffering some sort of multiple personality disorder, or that he had temporarily lost his bearings. One feels like crying out: 'Paul, which is it? Are you rich or poor? Do you possess everything or nothing? Which is it, because it can't be both? Well in Paul's mind it was both. The truth was he was often misjudged and dishonoured, people spread bad reports about him, sometimes he was near to death, beaten, sorrowful, poor, having nothing. *Yet* at the same time the complete opposite was happening. Paul lived in two dimensions. In this world he had pain and suffering, but God's kingdom had broken into his life. Rather like a science fiction movie the future kingdom had blown a hole into the present. So in the midst of poverty he experienced the riches of the future kingdom. In the midst of misery he experienced the joy of the future kingdom. And this was the secret of his stability. It's what kept him going when he was experiencing terrible adversity. Living a two-dimensional life is what will provide the 'ballast' when the storms rage around us.

Richard Wurmbrand was held by the Rumanian communists for fourteen years in solitary confinement. For part of that time he was kept in a cell which was three paces by three. Yet in that cell he danced for joy on many nights. He didn't mind if his captors thought he had gone mad, because he had discovered a beauty in Christ which he had not know before. Like Paul, Richard Wurmbrand had discovered the power of living a two-dimensional life.[10] Paul suffered hardship for most of his Christian life; Richard Wurmbrand for fourteen years. What was their secret?

How does one live conscious of God's kingdom when things are going wrong? It is one thing when the sun is shining and everything is going well, but another when we've just discovered our son, of so much promise, is on drugs, or our beautiful sixteen-year-old daughter is pregnant, or when our spouse has decided he doesn't love us anymore and has decided someone else is more attractive, or when the debts are mounting up and we can't see any way to pay them, or when our job is on the line, or when problems in the church are growing. Then it's very difficult to remember God's kingdom, let alone experience its presence in our lives. At that moment we need help to put the two-dimensional life into practice.

Focus on the Unseen

There are three keys which should enable us to keep our equilibrium whatever is happening around us. The first is found earlier in Paul's letter to the Corinthians. 'For our light and momentary troubles are achieving for us an eternal glory that far outweighs them all. So we fix our eyes, not on what is seen, but on what is unseen. For what is seen is temporary, but what is unseen is eternal.'[11] One of the keys to weathering the storms of life is our focus. We have a choice to focus either on the problems or on God's kingdom. Barbara Johnson encourages us to keep an *eternal perspective* as a way of coping with disappointment and heartache.

> There is no better way out of the cesspool than the rope of eternal perspective – knowing that 'THIS ISN'T IT.' What is happening is only temporary, and it will pass. Having an eternal perspective means keeping your rear-view mirror small and narrow and your windshield big and wide so that you can see farther down the road and look forward to what the future holds. True, you can't see the immediate future – tomorrow, next month, or even a few years from now. But you do know you will be a winner in the end.[12]

The reason, I believe, that Paul stressed fixing our eyes not on what is seen but on what is unseen, is because we need reminding to do the one, but we don't need reminding to do the other. When we have a difficult problem, or we are in pain we naturally focus on it. We don't need ourselves or anyone else to tell us to do so. I have a friend who was recently diagnosed with breast cancer. I don't think for one moment that she wakes up each morning and tells herself to focus on the cancer. When she opens her eyes her mind automatically goes to her point of concern. She needs no help or discipline to think about that. What she does have to discipline herself to do is to focus on the eternal things of God as well. It is good to remind ourselves that we can choose what we think about and we can change the way we feel by what we think.

Unless we make a decision to focus on the things of the kingdom, we will be overwhelmed by what is happening in the here and now. It is a case of fixing our eyes on the 'all things' of God which are not curtailed by time. There is no ending to them – they have no boundaries. They are eternal. Whereas the problems we are facing were born in time and will end in time. They have limits to them, and in comparison to eternity, time is very short. However, while we are in the middle of the suffering, it may seem like an eternity! So, practically, what does it mean to focus on the things of the kingdom?

Recently a young pastor shared with me his tendency to become emotionally embroiled in the problems of his church members. He said that he felt burdened by the responsibility for their development and happiness and was continually worried about them in case they grew discouraged and fell away. We talked about the Bible's attitude to problems; how even Jesus learned obedience through the things he suffered; how James wrote about difficulties developing maturity. Focusing in this way on biblical truths started to give the young man a different attitude to what was happening. Instead of being sucked into a cultural mind-set about happiness and quick answers, he began to see it God's way. Suddenly the problems took on a different appearance. In God's economy they now possessed the possibility of becoming positive agents for growth. The burden of responsibility, which was sapping his energy and joy, began to abate. It is only too easy to be influenced by the prevailing attitudes of the world and to lose one's focus on the eternal truths of God. When a biblical focus is regained we find ourselves rejoicing in God's purposes and are able to take a more objective view of what is happening.

When we have looked at every other avenue for dealing with the problem, and have drawn a blank, we may feel that we are left with no way out. But God always allows us a way of escape and this may be it. But to do this there is a proviso. It is impossible to focus with any sort of peace on the eternal things of God if we do not completely trust him.

Another biblical character who expressed his bewilderment and anger to God was Habakkuk. He lived in a time when wickedness, strife and oppression was rife in Judah. He was perplexed that God seemingly did nothing. The whole book is an account of Habakkuk arguing and wrestling with God. It starts:

How long, O LORD, must I call for help,
    but you do not listen?
Or cry out to you, 'Violence!'
    but you do not save?
Why do you make me look at injustice?

> Why do you tolerate wrong?
> Destruction and violence are before me;
>> there is strife, and conflict abounds.
> Therefore the law is paralysed,
>> and justice never prevails.
> The wicked hem in the righteous,
>> so that justice is perverted.[13]

Habakkuk could have been living at the beginning of the twenty-first century AD instead of 640–609 BC. We have all probably called out to God in this way when faced with unfairness and injustice. 'Oh God where are you? I have been calling out and you never answer me.' But God did answer the complaint. He said that he was going to use the Babylonians to execute judgement on Judah. The prophet was more perplexed than ever. How could God appoint such a wicked nation to execute his judgement? Once again God answered and in the middle of his explanation said something of great importance to Habakkuk. 'But the righteous will live by his faith.'[14] Paul echoed these words in his letter to the Romans. It was the phrase which changed Martin Luther's life and sparked the Reformation in the sixteenth century.

'He who has a why to live can bear with almost any how' (Nietzsche). In one sense the famous quote, from such a famous unbeliever, is true and Christians have found the ultimate answer to their question 'why'. However, in the context of suffering the question can never be answered with complete satisfaction. When a child dies, or a mother of four is diagnosed with terminal cancer, or we watch the genocide of a whole population on the television, there is no answer to the question 'why'.

In the end, after all the theological discussions and expla-
nations, there is only one response we can make. It is the
one God asked of Habakkuk. 'The righteous [my people]
will live by his faith [by trusting me].'

Trust God

God was asking Habakukk to trust him, in spite of his per-
plexity. This is the second key to stability. We have to trust
God. Each of these keys hang together. You can't have one
without the other. We are living in the reality of the two
worlds – the everyday world of the here and now, and the
kingdom of God which came with Jesus. We have to focus
on the kingdom and that's impossible to do if we don't
trust the King of that kingdom. We have already seen that
one trigger for negative feelings is a wrong view of God.
Before we can trust God we have to correct any misconceptions we may have of him. And to do this we have to
know the truth and speak this truth to ourselves. God is
not like our earthly father, nor is he like any other authority figure or abusive person we may have known. Sadly,
some people never move on to full commitment because of
their failure to correct such misconceptions. At a conference a few years ago I was asked to talk to a young girl of
about eighteen. She had collapsed in tears in a meeting,
saying she couldn't believe that God was a God of love. I
asked her why, and she told me that she had been raped
when she was fifteen and was angry with men, and with
God for allowing it to happen. Nothing I said seemed to
help her. For the rest of the week she continued to come
to all the meetings, sitting at the back in sullen silence.
Everyone who talked with her received the same response
as I had done. I feared she was going to leave a miserable

'victim'. But on the very last day of the conference, she suddenly caved in. In tears, she began to release forgiveness to the person who had raped her. She asked God to forgive her for holding such a grudge against God himself. She finally committed her life into God's hands and left the hall looking a different girl. So often there isn't such a happy ending. Some choose to remain the 'victim', which gives them an excuse not to trust anyone and certainly not God.

God is not like anyone we have ever known. He is totally 'other'.

God is Awesome

God is the Creator of everything, not just what we know and see, but of the whole universe and beyond. When we actually allow ourselves time to think about this, it is an awesome thought. Many years ago, when our eldest daughter was about nine years old, we travelled back to South America by boat. One clear, calm night in the middle of the Atlantic Ocean, David decided to take her up on deck to see the stars. He instructed her to look up and to admire God's handiwork. Charlotte stared up at the night sky, and after an awed silence burst into tears. She was so overwhelmed by the immensity of it that it was almost too much for her.

God is sovereign. If he wanted to destroy us he could do so in an instant. We cannot lift a finger without him. He holds everything together by his word. Without him we would disintegrate into millions of atoms. He is fearful and awesome and way beyond our questioning and understanding. Trying to comprehend God is as ridiculous as an ant trying to understand the M25, only more so!

Although it seems to take a long time to get to the point, the book of Job is helpful here. Job and his friends tried every way to understand and explain why Job was suffering in such a terrible manner. Job was convinced that he had done nothing to warrant the suffering he was going through, and he challenged God. 'I sign now my defence, let the Almighty answer me; let my accuser put his indictment in writing.' In the end God answered but said absolutely nothing about Job's suffering. Instead he drew Job's attention to his work of creation. 'Where were you when I laid the earth's foundation? Tell me, if you understand? Who marked off its dimensions? Surely you know! Who stretched a measuring line across it? On what were its footings set, or who laid its cornerstone – while the morning stars sang together and all the angels shouted for joy?' Just one question after another as God demonstrated the futility of man's attempt to understand him. The story ends with Job on his face before God. 'I know that you can do all things; no plan of yours can be thwarted. You asked, 'Who is this that obscures my counsel without knowledge?' All Job could answer was: 'Surely I spoke of things I did not understand, things too wonderful for me to know.'[15]

It is hard to envisage God as he really is because our minds are finite. As the Americans say when faced with something amazing, but incomprehensible, 'It is enough to blow the doors off your mind.' And that is exactly what we need: the doors to our mind blown off so that we don't limit God and box him in. He is limitless and cannot be confined by us, yet we shrink him and then wonder why we can't trust him and are constantly consumed by worry and frustration.

God Loves Us!

This amazing God loves us and knows us personally. In fact he has counted every hair on our head. Rather like a mother counts her new baby's fingers and toes, God counts our hairs. He doesn't just love us he adores us. He sings over us. He delights in us. And what is more he has a purpose for each of us. And like a mother who suffers every time her children are hurt God suffers with us and stretches out his arms to comfort us. Because he gave humanity free will he does not intervene in all we do. Instead he provides ways of healing; strengthening and comforting, and he can in a miraculous way, impossible to comprehend, turn the curses in our lives into blessings.[16]

The early days of the Christian church are a good example of this. After Stephen's martyrdom a great persecution broke out in Jerusalem and the people were scattered far and wide. At the time it must have seemed like a terrible tragedy to be uprooted from one's country and exiled, in many cases to a foreign land. But God in his infinite wisdom turned the apparent 'curse' into a 'blessing'. The ordinary men and women who were dispersed went everywhere preaching the word of God, and as a result a great number of people believed and turned to the Lord. In God's hands the tragedy was turned around and became the first great missionary movement.

Most importantly, if we doubt the love of God then we need to focus on Jesus. 'Look at Jesus and you see God's face wet with human tears and God's heart roused with outrage.'[17] Jesus said that if you have seen him you have seen the Father.[18]

This quote from Juan Arias shows how twisted our views of God can be.

No, I shall never believe in:

The God who catches man by surprise in a sin of
    weakness,
The God who condemns material things,
The God who loves pain,
The God who flashes a red light against human
    joys,
The God who makes himself feared,
The God who does not allow people to talk famil-
    iarly to him,
The grandfather-God whom one can twist around
    one's little finger,
The lottery-God whom one can find only by
    chance,
The judge-God who can give a verdict only with a
    rule book in his hands,
The God incapable of smiling at many of man's
    awkward mistakes,
The God who 'plays at' condemning,
The God who 'sends' people to hell,
The God who always demands 100 per cent in
    examinations,
The God who can be fully explained by a philoso-
    phy,
The God incapable of understanding that children
    will always get themselves dirty and be forgetful,
The God who demands that if a man is to believe
    he must give up being a man,
The God who does not accept a seat at our human
    festivities,
The God whom only the mature, the wise, or the

comfortably situated can understand,

The aseptic God thought up by so many theologians and canonists in their ivory towers,

The God who says, 'You will pay for that!'

The God who says and feels nothing about the agonizing problems of suffering humanity,

The God whose disciples turned their backs on the world's work and are indifferent to their brother's story,

The God who does not go out to meet the person who has abandoned him

The God incapable of making everything new,

The God who has never wept for men,

The God who is not light,

The God who prefers purity to love,

The God who is not present where (people) love each other,

The God in whom there is no mysteries, who is not greater than we are,

The God who, to make us happy, offers us a happiness divorced from our human nature,

The God who does not have the generosity of the sun, which warms everything it touches,

The God who is not love and who does not know how to transform into love everything he touches,

The God incapable of captivating man's heart,

The God who would not have become man, with all that implies,

The God in whom I cannot hope.

No, I shall never believe in such a God![19]

God Sees the Big Picture

Habakkuk saw what was happening in Judah while he lived there. God knew Judah's history from beginning to end; he had created the whole universe. Habakkuk lived for a brief time. God exists for all time. He is above all. He sees the big picture, more than we can ever comprehend. There is a parallel in the real-life police dramas we see on TV as we witness police at work. The police are called to the scene of a robbery in a high street bank. They arrive just as the robbers drive off in their stolen van. The police give chase, but the van is soon lost to sight. Suddenly a voice comes through on the radio. It's 'the eye in the sky'. The helicopter, circling above the police car, can see the big picture and guides the police in their chase. The direction they are told to go in may seem crazy to the police but they have to trust that the men in the helicopter can see the whole scenario and know where the robbers' van is heading. In the same way we have to trust God in our times of pain, disappointment, illness and loss because he is the God of the big picture.

Even though Habakkuk was still seeing devastation he made a decision to trust God. Trusting is simply a decision of the will. We decide something despite the circumstances. That's faith! This is the only time we will have the opportunity to use faith – there'll be no need for faith in eternity. We will either understand it all, or we will be so caught up in the glory that we won't need to!

Someone discovered the following verse written on the cell wall of a concentration camp.

I believe in the sun,
    Even when it is not shining.

> I believe in love,
> Even when I feel it not.
> I believe in God,
> Even when He is silent.

Habakkuk made his decision and with a beautiful song of praise demonstrated his trust, even as he anticipated the devastation which would result from the coming invasion. This brings us to the third key.

Review

1. How would you change the description of your present circumstances to include a second dimension?
2. Right now, in what situation is God asking you to trust him? Can you do that? Or does your view of him hinder you?

Nine

THE POWER OF PRAISE

The Jews in Habakkuk's day were going through a tough time and God's challenge to them to was to live by faith. There was in fact nothing new about this. They had been called to a life of faith since the days of Abraham who had left Ur of the Chaldeans not knowing where he was going. He just had to trust that God had a place for him.[1] As a result of the challenge Habakkuk made an amazing response to God:

> Though the fig-tree does not bud
>   and there are no grapes on the vines,
> though the olive crop fails
>   and the fields produce no food,
> though there are no sheep in the pen
>   and no cattle in the stalls,
> yet I will rejoice in the LORD
>   I will be joyful in God my Saviour.[2]

This is one of the strongest affirmations of faith in all Scripture, according to the NIV Study Bible.

Learning to praise God despite our circumstances is the most powerful tool of all. Our days on this planet will be littered with difficult situations which can cause us a lot of pain and stimulate feelings of fear, anxiety, anger and sadness. These invade and complicate our lives. We have already examined several ways of alleviating these feelings and whether these are effective or not this last suggestion should have priority. In fact it is not even an option; it's a 'biblical must'. If we can bring ourselves to put it into practice we will find it the most effective tool of all.

Giving Thanks

Giving thanks to God, in the middle of distress and our questions about it, is the ultimate in trust. It says to God. 'Even though it's beyond my understanding, I trust you as my sovereign God. You see everything from beginning to end. You love me and have my best interests at heart' – this is faith and by faith we stand firm.[3]

Giving Thanks Without Hypocrisy

But we say to ourselves: 'When I am in the middle of the most unbelievable pain isn't it hypocrisy to give thanks? Isn't it unreal?' When I first read books telling me to praise God for everything, even my suffering, I found it very hard to swallow. Os Guinness says that when an experience is considered in terms of its overall character, our appropriate response to God is unreserved trust and thanksgiving. There is no situation so evil that it is beyond redeeming by God. From this perspective it is always right to trust God and give thanks.

However, he goes on to say that if we think of the same experience in terms of its different parts, it may well include things that are evil, painful and disappointing. We should respond appropriately to each of these individual elements, and in many instances our response should not be thanks. Outrage is appropriate in response to genuine wrongs, tears in response to grief, shock in response to unexpected disaster. We mustn't force ourselves to thank God for these things or we will be harder on ourselves and softer on evil than God is. It is not even that Christians need not give thanks for these things, but that Christians especially should not give thanks for them. We should always be as human as God made us.[4]

Certainly Jesus did not thank God for the money-changers in the temple, nor did he thank God that Jerusalem had rejected him, nor that he was going to his death in terrible agony of body and soul. Yet Jesus was a thankful person and there are many times in the Bible when we find him giving thanks. At the Last Supper when he took the bread and then the cup he first gave thanks and offered it to the disciples, saying, 'Drink from it, all of you. This is my blood of the covenant, which is poured out for many for the forgiveness of sins. I tell you, I will not drink of this fruit of the vine from now on until that day when I drink it anew with you in my Father's kingdom.'[5] He was facing the crucifixion, the prospect of which was to cause him bitter anguish of soul, and yet he could give thanks because at the same time he rejoiced in God's overall plan of redemption.

When thanking God it is easier to do what Paul told the Thessalonians to do. 'Be joyful always; pray continually; give thanks in all circumstances, for this is God's will for you in Christ Jesus.'[6] It doesn't say 'for' all circumstances. It says in' all circumstances. Whatever we may be going through God is still God so we can render to him our praise and thanksgiving. In fact we have a duty to do so. If the Queen came to visit, we would greet her with proper respect because of who she is, even if we had a bad headache. So whatever is wrong in our lives God is still the

King of kings and worthy of our praise.

A number of years ago when we were facing several difficult situations at once, I bumped into a friend and shared with her our troubles. She was very understanding and sympathetic. It was good; I felt understood. Sympathy is always sweet! Later that afternoon I had to drive a distance to speak at an evening meeting. I started driving down the M25, but I had not been driving long when I began to feel very depressed. All the energy seemed to have seeped out of me. As I prayed that God would give me strength I began to remember my conversation of the afternoon. I had spoken the truth to my friend. Life was difficult right then. But as I thought about it I realised that it had only been half the truth. Life was difficult but that didn't alter the fact that God was still good and his love still endured for ever. Like Paul in his letter to the Corinthians, the two truths had to operate together. Both were equally true and I had only focused on one. So for the rest of the journey I praised God, singing and giving him thanks for who he is. I found the depression lifted and my energy returned.

So there is no hypocrisy in praising God 'in' every situation. However, Paul also tells the Ephesians always to give thanks to God the Father 'for' everything, in the name of our Lord Jesus Christ.[7] Hard as we may find it there is a sense in which we also have to give God thanks 'for' everything, as well as 'in' everything. The one is easier to understand and put into practice, while the other may seem like dishonesty. Yet if God is God, then he is Lord of our suffering also. Catherine Marshall's little granddaughter, Amy Catherine, died even though she was sure it would have been God's will to heal her.

I saw Satan's work all over the physical problem, the tiny, genetically damaged body. And just as steadily, I was refusing to see God 'in' the situation at all. So I had been attributing Amy's death to the combined factors of our failure in prayer plus the power of evil. Seeing it that way, I had not been able to receive the baby's death as from God's hands in a greater scheme of things not yet given to me to understand. It was a shock to realise that as a result of this defective thinking I had actually ascribed more power to evil than to God.[8]

When we fail to see God 'in' everything, in fact we are attributing more power to someone or something else. When we thank God for suffering we are telling him we trust him as God Almighty – one who on occasions permits pain to enter our lives for reasons we cannot understand. So although I would still find it hard to thank God for a cancer that had invaded a small child's body, I could thank him that the life of the child was in his tender care, that he understood the parents' anguish, that he would never leave them nor forsake them, and could bring good out of apparent evil. I would thank him that nothing could thwart his will. And I would pray for his kingdom to come and his will be done in that situation.

As we make an effort to use this tool in dealing with negative feelings, we may need some help to stimulate us into action. There are a variety of reasons why we should give God thanks, whatever is happening to us, and whatever we may be feeling.

It's God's Will

Paul urges the Christians at Thessalonica to 'Be joyful always; pray continually; give thanks in all circumstances, for this is God's will for you in Christ Jesus.'[9] We frequently pray that God's will may be done in our lives but don't always follow this injunction. I like the story of Billy Bray, a Cornish miner who came to Christ in the last century after a life of debauchery and drunkenness. He was well known for always praising God in a very noisy manner. On one occasion he went to visit a dying saint, whose character had been unblemished for many years, but whose natural disposition was modest and retiring almost to a fault. The dying saint was just on the verge of heaven and could only speak in a whisper. He said, 'I wish I had a voice so that I might praise the Lord!' 'You should have praised him, my brother, when you had one,' was Billy's quiet comment. Another time when he heard of the triumphant death of another saint, who died shouting 'Victory!' Billy's heart was so touched he shouted, 'Glory! If a dying woman praised the Lord, I should think a living man might.'

Billy took literally the injunction to: 'Rejoice evermore – Pray without ceasing – In everything give thanks.' In his opinion a Christian might be poor, but it was his duty to 'rejoice evermore'; afflicted, but still he must 'rejoice evermore; tempted and tried and persecuted, but he must notwithstanding, 'rejoice evermore'. He always seemed able to smile through his tears. The sickness of a child, the death of a wife, would not silence his voice, or repress his joy. It is said that when his wife died he was so overpowered with the thought of his 'dear Joey' having escaped from earth's toils and sufferings to the rest and bliss of heaven, that he began to jump and dance about the room exclaiming, 'Bless the Lord! My dear Joey is gone up with the bright ones! Glory! Glory! In bad times he would say, 'We have a little bitter, but it is mixed with a great deal of sweet.'[10]

Praise and thanksgiving have a very prominent place in Scripture and many of the New Testament letters contain similar encouragement to be joyful and thankful in every situation. Obviously God wants us to adopt this attitude. In fact Scripture even states that: 'A cheerful heart is good medicine, but a crushed spirit dries up the bones.'[11] This is thought to have been written in the tenth century BC, but it is only now at the beginning of the twenty-first century AD that some medical societies are investigating laughter and smiles for clinical benefits. In fact a recent discovery has found that both laughing and crying stimulate endorphins, pain-killing hormones.[12]

A thankful attitude benefits us spiritually and physically and it seems that socially and mentally it has a positive effect also. It creates a better mood and feeds hope. For example, it has been found that good moods enhance the ability to think flexibly and with more complexity, thus making it easier to find solutions to problems, whether intellectual or interpersonal. People in good moods have a perceptual bias that leads them to be more expansive and positive in their thinking. Modern researchers also found that hope is beneficial. It does more than offer a bit of solace amid affliction; it plays a surprisingly potent role in life, offering an advantage in realms as diverse as school achievement and bearing up in onerous jobs.[13]

The most persuasive reason for being thankful is that it is God's will. But it is also logical, considering who God is and what he has done for us.

It is Reasonable

Let the peace of Christ rule in your hearts, since as members of one body you were called to peace. And be thankful. Let the word of Christ dwell in you richly as you teach and admonish one another with all wisdom, and as you sing psalms, hymns and spiritual songs with gratitude in your hearts to God. And whatever you do, whether in word or deed, do it all in the name of the Lord Jesus, giving thanks to God the Father through him.[14]

It is reasonable that we should be grateful to God. He has given us life and provided us with all we need for life. He has sent his only begotten Son, Jesus, to make a way to heaven for us. He has given us eternal life. Everything we have comes from him. How can we not be thankful and give him praise. Chuck Irish, an American priest, has created his own definition of praise and worship.

Praise is the physical and verbal response to the presence of and our experience of God. Worship is our surrender to God. Praise, thus, can be expressed in a variety of ways: song, words, painting, dance, instruments, and good works. Worship is when we surrender our selves, souls, bodies, and possessions to the will of God. Praise and worship go hand in hand.[15]

The Psalms are full of God's praises. King David, often afflicted and tormented, never seems to have run out of words with which to praise God. When we lack inspiration we can do no better than turn to the Psalms. We can easily make some of the psalms of gratitude our own. 'You turned my wailing into dancing; you removed my sackcloth and clothed me with joy, that my heart may sing to you and not be silent. O LORD my God, I will give you thanks for ever.'[16]

Similarly, though Paul was a man who knew many hardships in his life, he was constantly thankful and encouraged other Christians to be the same. In particular he was thankful for Jesus and the privileges that came through him. 'But thanks be to God! He gives us the victory through our Lord Jesus Christ.'[17] 'But thanks be to God, who always leads us in triumphal procession in Christ and through us spreads everywhere the fragrance of the knowledge of him.'[18] 'But thanks be to God for his indescribable gift!'[19] For Paul, Jesus was that indescribable gift. Like Paul, our only possible response, whatever our situation, is gratitude for a gift that beggars description. Praise is the fruit of a grateful heart.

It is the Fruit of our Lips

'Through Jesus, therefore, let us continually offer to God a sacrifice of praise – the fruit of lips that confess his name.'[20] Fruit! That's what praise is. So long as a Christian is attached to the Vine he should produce fruit – fruit of many different kinds which bring glory to God, such as love, joy, peace, kindness, longsuffering and patience. The fruit of praise is expressed in words with which we bless God.

When there is very little praise in a person's life, one would wonder at the reality of his faith. It's back to Billy

Bray again! No one who lived in Cornwall in Billy's time would have had any doubt about his faith. Though just a poor miner he was rich in magnifying the Lord. It seemed that he could hardly help himself. He was bursting with exuberant praise. Even when others would have waited first, to see how things turned out before they praised God, Billy would praise God anyway. A good friend once said to him that the Lord had told him to give him a coat and waistcoat, but he wasn't sure if it would fit. 'If the Lord told you to give them to me, they will fit me all right, for He knows my size exactly.' It was Billy's opinion that almost all the garments which he had given to him fitted him so well because 'he and fashion had once quarrelled', and the breach had never been made up.[21]

On another occasion, Billy was looking for something he could use for a pulpit in a little chapel he had built. He found a three-cornered cupboard at an auction which he thought would do. Someone gave him six shillings and Billy bid for the cupboard. But Billy knew nothing of auctions and eager to have his pulpit he immediately offered his six shillings. But someone bid seven shillings and to Billy's surprise he lost his cupboard. 'I'll be down and tell Father about it,' said Billy and started off for the little chapel. On his way he saw his cupboard going up the hill so he followed it. The man who bought it carried it to his house and then found he couldn't get it through the door. Billy was delighted. 'I'll give 'e six shillin' for un, if you'll carry un down to my little chapel.' The man did so willingly. 'Bless the Lord!' cried Billy, ' 'tis just like Him. He knew I couldn't carry un myself, so He got this man to carry un for me.' He saw God in every situation and praises just poured out of his mouth. He used to say: 'If they were to put me in a barrel, I would shout glory out through the bunghole! Praise the Lord!'

It would be tempting to think thanksgiving and praise an easy option when we read of men like Billy Bray. There is no doubt that the goodness of God makes us grateful and that in turn produces the fruit of praise. But when hardship and heartache come our way it's difficult to be grateful, and then praise is far from our lips. Which is why it is also a sacrifice.

It is a Sacrifice

'. . . let us continually offer to God a sacrifice of praise.'[22] It will not be easy to put this into practice, but when we do it will change our lives. Thanking God in a difficult situation is like a relinquishment. At that moment we are surrendering to God's will and purposes. We are confessing that he is an infinite being, far greater than ourselves; that his ways and his understanding are way above ours. This act of surrender brings with it surprising joy. When Barbara Johnson's son, Larry, disappeared into a gay lifestyle, she was heartbroken. For a year she sank into deep depression and then one day she suddenly decided she must relinquish her son to God and in her imagination she nailed him to the cross. She said to God: 'Whatever, Lord, whatever happens, I'm nailing him to the Cross and giving him to you.' . . . When she said, 'Whatever, Lord,' she said that it released a million little splashes of joy deep inside of her. Her teeth stopped itching, the shag rug in her throat disappeared, the elephant that had been sitting on her chest for nearly a year was gone, and so was that knife twisting there close to her heart.[23]

Many years ago when our children were all small a

friend printed a notice for me in large letters. I placed it behind the sink where it was constantly in view. The notice read: Halleluya Anyway! Despite the nappies, nits and noise, I was determined that I would praise God. But I needed the notice, because at times it was very hard to remember to be thankful. It is not even a case of not wanting to, it is just that the situation sometimes demands so much attention, and the feelings are screaming so loudly that they drown out any thoughts of being thankful.

C.T. Studd, the great missionary pioneer, used to have a notice in his compound in Africa which read: 'Grumblers go home. Only gamblers wanted here.' When we were on the mission field I had a lot of sympathy with the 'grumblers'! Moans come naturally to the lips when things get hard, which they inevitably do, in more primitive conditions and far from home. When things are tough it is only discipline and decision that will keep us praising God. After a while a habit will be formed and it won't be quite so difficult. Matthew Henry was a well-known Bible commentator. One day he was robbed, and reading the careful entry in his dairy makes one realise that being thankful takes some deliberate thought. 'Let me be thankful – first, because I was never robbed before. Second, because although, they took my wallet they did not take my life. Third, because although they took my all, it was not much. And fourth, because it was I who was robbed, not I who robbed.'[24]

The prophet Daniel displayed great discipline when he was taken into captivity to Babylon. He refused to be defiled by eating all the rich food and wine he was offered. He was also careful to keep the law of God. So, when trying to trap him, the jealous officials of Babylon realised that the only way would be if it had something to do with the law of his God. They managed to get King Darius to issue an edict that no one should pray to any god or man during the next thirty days except to the king. Whoever broke that law was to be thrown into the lions' den. 'Now when Daniel learned that the decree had been published, he went home to his upstairs room where the windows opened towards Jerusalem. Three times a day he got down on his knees and prayed, giving thanks to his God, just as he had done before.'[25] Everything was stacked against him. It must have taken a stubborn determination to give God thanks in that situation, but Daniel had already formed a discipline. He gave thanks – just as he had done every day before. Once a habit is formed it is not easily broken. 'Dare to be a Daniel!'

Moses clearly states that curses will follow those who are not grateful. 'Because you did not serve the LORD your God joyfully and gladly in the time of prosperity, therefore in hunger and thirst, in nakedness and dire poverty, you will serve the enemies the Lord sends against you. He will put an iron yoke on your neck until he has destroyed you.'[25] It's a grim warning to those of us who find it easier to give way to our natural desire to groan and moan, rather than make the sacrifice to be thankful. However, awaiting us there are some wonderful blessings when we do make the effort.

Review

1. What place does praise and thanksgiving have in your life?
2. How could you help yourself to become a more thankful person?

Ten

THE FRUIT OF THANKSGIVING

Praising God in all the circumstances of our lives, both when we are down and when we are up, means there will be consequences. The beneficial results will be largely experienced personally, but they will most certainly have a ripple effect socially. Our lives touch others, whether we are aware of it or not. 'No man is an island.'

A Social Lift

'A happy heart makes the face cheerful, but heartache crushes the spirit.'[1] It is difficult to be thankful and look miserable at the same time and a cheerful face is infectious, lifting the spirit of others. When I was a new Christian our church went to sing carols at a Rest Home for the elderly. Talking to the residents afterwards I met Mary, a lady in her eighties. When she learned we had the same name she was delighted. Her company was like a tonic to the soul. Despite being old and frail she was cheerful and chatty. Although the difference in our ages must have been more than sixty years I couldn't resist her company and from that time until I left Oxford I visited her every week. There was nothing sacrificial in my visits. I did it because I was blessed every time I saw her smiling face. Our attitude to life affects other people, whether we like it or not. Therefore our thankfulness will rub off on other people.

Emotional Stability

Another consequence of thankfulness will be the fact that our circumstances will not have the power to control us emotionally in the same way as previously. When circumstances are getting us down it is easy to feel taken over by them. We experience swings of mood, like being on a roller-coaster. When our 'out of work' spouse applies for work, we wait anxiously for the replies to his applications – one day hopeful, the next despairing. When the replies come we soar emotionally if he has been called for an interview, and then plunge back into despair when he doesn't get the job. This is when we realise we are being controlled by the circumstances. When we change our thoughts and prayers to ones of praise and thanksgiving whatever the replies we gradually find ourselves back in the driving seat of our emotions.

Oprah Winfrey, the talk show hostess, said on one of her shows that she had recently changed the way she kept her dairy. Previously she had made more negative entries than positive ones, but now she had decided to write five things for which she was grateful every day. She said that it had revolutionised her whole life.

Certainly we have found that being thankful has had a stabilising effect upon our family and our personal lives. One particular incident stands out in our memories. While living in Chile we moved many times. Our last move was a memorable one. We had been given notice to quit our rented accommodation and were urgently seeking for somewhere to go. The Diocese wanted to buy a suitable house for us, but it was at a time when there was little on the market. One day I was at the bakery and someone mentioned a house they thought was up for sale. I ran home quickly and collected the family. We drove round to the address we had been given. As we turned the corner and saw the house my heart leapt. 'This is it,' I thought. The children squealed with delight. We all fell in love with it at first sight. It looked so friendly and inviting. We rang the bell and the six of us stood on the doorstep hopefully. The owners were a little surprised to see complete strangers standing before them and when we explained why we were there, they shook their heads. They had no intention of moving. We got back in the car feeling foolish and disappointed. On the way home the girls were expressing their feelings, when David said he thought that we ought to thank God for what had happened. 'We can't do that,' they shouted. 'We wanted that house.' David explained to them that we can always thank God because he knows what he is doing, and we can thank him that we have an opportunity to trust him more. So that is what we did. Quietly and with little enthusiasm we began to thank him. But gradually we got into the swing of it and by the time we reached home we were all quite cheerful, despite the urgency of the situation.

But that was not the end of the story. The reason our family will never forget the experience is because by the end of that week we were in the house of our dreams. The owner of that friendly little house was suddenly requested, by his firm, to move to the capital by the following week. He immediately rang us and asked if we could move quickly into his house, rent free, so that it would not be left empty. He said that when his future was clearer we could arrange whether to rent or buy it. In fact we stayed for six months in the house without paying rent and then the Diocese was able to buy it. We lived there until we

finally came back to England. 'Delight yourself in the
LORD and he will give you the desires of your heart.'[2]

Writing from prison in Rome (in prison – imagine it!)
Paul actually told the Philippians not to be 'anxious about
anything, but in everything, by prayer and petition, with
thanksgiving, present your requests to God. And the peace
of God, which transcends all understanding, will guard
you hearts and your minds in Christ Jesus.'[3] The result of
prayer with thanksgiving, he said, would be a peaceful
heart instead of an anxious one. A few verses on he makes
his famous declaration: 'For I have learned to be content
whatever the circumstances. I know what it is to be in
need, and I know what it is to have plenty. I have learned
the secret of being content in any and every situation,
whether well fed or hungry, whether living in plenty or in
want. I can do everything through him who gives me
strength.'[4] Peacefulness and contentment are the fruits of
a thankful heart. They are certainly not dependent upon
there being tranquillity and peace around us. They can be
experienced even in the middle of turmoil.

I recently read a delightful story of a king who once
offered a prize to the artist who could paint the best picture depicting peace. Many artists tried but when the king
looked at all the pictures there were only two he liked.
One was the picture of a calm lake. The lake perfectly mir-
rored the peaceful mountains all around. It was certainly a
picture of serene tranquillity. The other picture was of
rugged, bare mountains, down the sides of which crashed
a foaming waterfall. The sky above was angry, the rain fell
and the lightning flashed. The picture did not reflect peace
at all. But when the king looked closely, he saw behind the
waterfall a tiny bush growing in a crack in the rock. In the

bush a mother bird had built her nest. There, in the midst of the torrent of angry water, sat the mother bird on her nest – in perfect peace. The king chose the second picture: 'Because,' he explained, 'peace does not mean to be in a place where there is no noise, trouble, or hard work. Peace means to be in the midst of all those things and still to be calm in your heart. That is the real meaning of peace.'[5] A thankful heart results in that sort of peace. 'Let the peace of Christ rule in your hearts, since as members of one body you were called to peace. And be thankful.'[6]

Dr Norman Vincent Peal of New York once received a letter from a lady who had been full of fear and worry. She wrote:

> My greatest progress dates from the night you told me that 'every day is a good day if you pray.' I began to put into practice the idea of affirming that this would be a good day the minute I woke up in the morning, and I can positively say that I haven't had a bad or upsetting day since that time . . . My days actually haven't been any smoother or any more free from petty annoyances than they ever were, but they just don't seem to have the power to upset me anymore. Every night I begin my prayers by listing all the things for which I am grateful, little things that happened during the day which added to the happiness of my day . . .[7]

A close relation to praise and thanksgiving is laughter. It has the same effect as thankfulness. Barbara Johnson tells a little story about her friend Marilyn whose mother had died and was cremated as requested. When Marilyn and her husband went to collect the remains, she said it was eerie. All her life she had known her mother in her earthly, physical state, now here were her 'cremains' being given to her in a shoe box! As she got into the car and joined her husband, clutching the shoe box, she could tell he felt awkward. The whole thing was becoming too grim and hard to bear. Placing the shoe box on the back seat she had a strong desire to lighten the moment, so she leaned over and said: 'Mom, do you need a seat belt?' '*Marilyn*!' was all her husband could say. But nevertheless it did the trick and their spirits were lifted. 'It wasn't that I was being irreverent about my mother,' she explained, 'or her "cremains". It was just for those few seconds I needed to lighten the moment and feel that I had a measure of control rather than having the circumstances control me.'

Barbara Johnson goes on to urge folks to keep a joy box of mementos – cards, clippings and little knick-knacks of every imaginable description, all of which can bring a smile, or even a chuckle, especially when they are feeling discouraged. Little things that bring back happy memories.[8]

Naturally Two-Dimensional

We started this book asking ourselves what would keep us from capsizing when the storms of life rage around us. A good part of the answer lies right here, in the power of praise and thanksgiving. As we develop a lifestyle of thanksgiving we will find we are naturally becoming two-dimensional people. Like Billy Bray we won't be able to help ourselves. 'I can't help praising the Lord as I go along the street. I lift one foot and it seems to say "Glory!" and I lift up the other and it seems to say "Amen", and so they keep on like that all the time I am walking.'[9] Without becoming 'too heavenly-minded to be any earthly good!' we will find that the future kingdom has blown a hole right into our present everyday lives. We may still be living in 'a Good Friday world' with all its pain and suffering but we will know, without a shadow of a doubt, that the victory of the resurrection will have become a part of our lives whatever the circumstances.

There was so much suffering in John Wimber's life, and towards the end it all just intensified. He knew what is was to live in 'a Good Friday' world, but he also knew what it was to be an 'Easter person'. One day, near the end of his life, his son Chris, who was dying of brain cancer, fell while John watched helplessly, unable to help his son get to his feet. Carol started to worry about how John must be feeling and thinking it would help him to talk about it, asked him how he had felt. He didn't even pause to think about it. He said with a look of awe and wonder on his face, 'I see the glory of God, Carol – think about it. Think about our whole life together. When has God not glorified himself?' Carol said that she didn't really understand what he meant at the time. Even as she wrote the book she still wasn't sure she knew, but whatever he meant, she knew that he had a better thing going than she did and she wasn't going to mess with it.[10]

More Glory
After Solomon built the temple in Jerusalem the great day came when the Ark of the Lord was brought into the temple.

All the Levites who were musicians . . . stood on the

east side of the altar, dressed in fine linen and playing cymbals, harps and lyres. They were accompanied by 120 priests sounding trumpets. The trumpeters and singers joined in unison, as with one voice, to give praise and thanks to the LORD. Accompanied by trumpets, cymbals and other instruments, they raised their voices in praise to the Lord and sang:

>He is good,
>>his love endures for ever.

Then the temple of the LORD was filled with a cloud, and the priests could not perform their service because of the cloud, for the glory of the LORD filled the temple of God.[11]

It must have been an amazing experience to see all those priests overcome by the presence of God, unable to continue playing their instruments, because of the glory of God.

When our mouths are filled more with gratitude than with grumbles then we will see God's glory in a way that will amaze us. I recently heard Mike Breen from St. Thomas' Church in Sheffield tell of an incredible experience he had had in Nigeria. He attended an all-night prayer meeting in Lagos of more than a million people, in a building one and a half kilometres long and three quarters of a kilometre wide. He was completely amazed by what he saw. He asked God what the difference was between there and back home, and the Lord seemed to say to him that there was no difference in anointing, it was just a different commitment. When he asked what was the difference in commitment he felt God say it was thanksgiving and testimony. So Mike said to the Lord, 'If it's thanksgiving I need to learn then teach me how to be thankful.' A day later he went down with a mysterious illness. He was extremely ill and eventually ended up in a hospital where they shook their heads at his condition, suspecting that he had contracted a serious tropical disease. Whatever it was they reckoned he would not be able to move on for another three weeks at least. During the night God reminded him of his request. So he began to be thankful. At first he couldn't think of anything to be thankful for. Then he began with the obvious things. The bed that was too small for his length, the little Pentecostal nurse who had prayed for him, for his family back in England, for his church, for his friends. All through the night he went on thanking God for everything he could think of. When the nurse came in the morning his temperature had returned to normal and he was perfectly well. He got up, showered and went to have a large breakfast! God had taught him how to be thankful and in the process he had seen the glory of God. The night I heard him tell that story, his audience of about 4,000 began to praise and thank God; very shortly afterwards God began to move in power. People were healed, anointed, oil began to drip off people's hands, a fragrance of roses hung in the air. As we acknowledged that God is good and his love endures for ever, his presence came and we were all filled with awe.

We shall see more of his glory, but best of all more of his glory will be seen in us. God himself inhabits the praises of his people.[12] In the act of praising and thanking God we are lifting him up, and enthroning him. Our praises are an acknowledgement that he is Lord of our lives. Spurgeon, the great nineteenth-century preacher, once said that God is most glorified in us when we are most satisfied in him. At first it might seem a struggle to thank him when we don't feel like it, but as we persevere it will gather momentum. We will find we become intoxicated with the goodness of God. Then God's glory starts to come through. And this is what God purposed for all of us, that we might live our lives to the praise of his glory.[13]

More of His Victory

When Jehoshaphat was King of Judah he took the people to fight against Moab and Ammon, who had vast armies. Jehoshaphat was clearly anxious about the coming battle so he enquired of the Lord. The prophetic word came back from Jahaziel that they were not to be afraid or discouraged because of the vast army, for the battle was not theirs, but God's. He told him that they would not have to fight the battle, but they were just to stand firm and see the deliverance that the Lord would give them. Their response to this word from God was to praise him with a loud voice. Then King Jehoshaphat placed men

> to sing to the LORD and to praise him for the splendour of his holiness as they went out at the head of the army saying:
>
> > 'Give thanks to the LORD
> > For his love endures for ever.'
>
> As they began to sing and praise, the LORD set ambushes against the men of Ammon and Moab .

... and they were defeated. Judah never had to fight the battle.[14]

God fought it for them, while they sang his praises!

Give thanks in all circumstances, for this is God's will for you. God wants to fight the battle of our circumstances for us. It is his desire to see us gain the victory over our negative emotions which hassle us and wear us out. The road to victory is paved with praise and thanksgiving.

When Paul and Silas were in Philippi they had a set-to with a slave girl, who was pestering them. They finally cast an evil spirit out of her which made the owners of the girl furious. They seized Paul and Silas and took them before the magistrates. The magistrates ordered them to be stripped, beaten and thrown into prison; the jailer was commanded to guard them carefully. At about midnight Paul and Silas were praying and singing hymns to God. Suddenly there was such a violent earthquake that the foundations of the prison were shaken. All the prison doors flew open and everybody's chains came loose. The poor jailer thought he was about to lose all the prisoners as well as his life. But Paul calmed him telling him they were all there. The jailer came trembling before Paul and asked him what he must do to be saved. That night he accepted Christ and he and his whole family were baptised.[15]

So often our circumstances and our negative emotions can act like prison bars. We feel as if there is no escape from them. When we start to praise him and thank him, despite the way we feel, we will be amazed at the miracles God will perform for us.

Review

1. In what circumstances do you find it difficult to praise God.
2. Make a list of things that you could praise God for in those circumstances.
3. In what areas of your life is God not being glorified?
4. Is praise a daily part of your life?

CONCLUSION

' As Christians how do we handle the painful feelings, which often enter our lives as unwelcome guests?' This is the question we started with.

Just the other day a man told us of a painful experience of being unjustly accused in a public forum by another Christian pastor. We knew he was speaking the truth, having heard it from another source also. His desire was to find a way of handling the situation in a godly and humble way. In fact his attitude was that he wanted to get as much benefit out of the situation as possible. In other words, whatever God wanted to teach him, he wanted to learn. Therefore he saw it as vitally important that he should react in the right way, despite the natural anger that he felt at the injustice of the situation.

This is the crunch. As Christians we do not have the same options open to us as the 'unsaved man in the street'. We have been called to travel 'a road less travelled' and a narrow one at that. But as we seek to handle our negative emotions God's way we grow and mature in the process. Sometimes the situation demands action, but oft times we are stuck in circumstances where the only change possible is a change of attitude – our attitude!

Jesus challenged his followers to deny themselves and take up the cross and follow him. Dying to self is a painful process, and dealing with our difficult feelings, in the ways suggested, will sometimes be like dying. Seeking God's kingdom first above our natural inclinations will be hard.

Giving thanks in all our circumstances will sometimes be a sacrifice; easy when life is going smoothly, but when we face injustice, rejection, loss or pain, we balk at the idea. Our natural reaction is to moan and groan. But if we can practise giving thanks despite our negative feelings, we will find a gradual change taking place. Instead of the turmoil there will be peace; instead of sadness, joy; instead of hatred, love. In the middle of the trial we will experience a 'kingdom breakthrough', which will give us a foretaste of future glory.

> Turn your eyes upon Jesus,
> Look full in His wonderful face,
> And the things of earth
> Will grow strangely dim
> In the light of His glory and Grace.[1]

NOTES

Chapter One

1. Carol Wimber, *The Way it Was* (London: Hodder & Stoughton, 1999).
2. Job 5:7
3. Barbara Johnson, *Splashes Of Joy in the Cesspools of Life* (Milton Keynes, Word Publishing, 1992).
4. Henri Nouwen, *The Inner Voice of Love* (London: Darton, Longman and Todd, 1997) p ix.
5. Christian Life Training, 1090 N Batavia, Orange, CA 92867 USA.
6. Barbara Johnson, *Splashes of Joy in the Cesspools of Life*, op. cit. p 8.
7. Susan Jeffers, *Feel the Fear and Do it Anyway* (London: Arrow Books, 1991) p 159.
8. Daniel Goleman, *Emotional Intelligence* (London: Bantam Books, 1995) p 56.
9. Ephesians 4:26
10. *Health & Safety Executive* (1997) *Health and Safety Statistics*, 1996/7, HSE Books, Sudbury.
11. *Telegraph* Magazine, 4.6.99.
12. Victor Frankl, *Man's Search for Meaning* (Beacon Press, 1993).

Chapter Two

1. Daniel Goleman, *Emotional Intelligence* (London: Bantam Books, 1995) p 289.
2. Ibid p 8.
3. Ibid p 294.
4. Ibid p 6.
5. *Daily Telegraph*, July 29, 1999.
6. Daniel Goleman, *Emotional Intelligence*, op. cit. p 21.
7. Ibid p 56.

Chapter Three

1. John Powell, S.J., *The Christian Vision* (T. More Press, 1996).
2. Daniel Goleman, *Emotional Intelligence* (London: Bantam Books, 1995) pp 20, 21.
3. Gordon MacDonald, *When Men Think Private Thoughts* (Milton Keynes: Thomas Nelson, 1996) p 24.

4. Chris Spicer, *Eight Characteristics of Highly Effective Christians* (Crowborough: Monarch, 1996) p 30.
5. Article in *Daily Telegraph* by Roger Highfield (Science Editor) 20.7.99.
6. Urie Bronfenbrenner, at Cornell University 24.9.93, quoted in Daniel Goleman, *Emotional Intelligence*, op. cit.p 234.
7. Daniel Goleman, *Emotional Intelligence*, op. cit. p xiii.
8. Industrial Society, *Managing Best Practice*, No.18 – Managing Stress
9. Heard at a lecture on Counselling Those with Psychological and Personality Disorders at Waverley Abbey Christian Training Centre.
10. Proverbs 13:12
11. Mark 8:27–33
12. Luke 24:10,11
13. Isaiah 55:8
14. Acts 1:6
15. Numbers 12:6–8
16. 1 Corinthians 13:12
17. Luke 2:19
18. Philippians 4:11–13
19. Romans 8:28

Chapter Four

1. Source: A. Faulkner, et al, *Knowing Our Own Minds*, Mental Health Foundation (1997).
2. Barbara Johnson, *Splashes of Joy* (Milton Keynes: Word Publications, 1992) p 37.
3. Olivia Tims and Lorraine Fraser, 'Tearful Chemistry', *The Times*, 18.7.86.
4. Dr Arthur Janov, *Prisoners of Pain* (Doubleday and Company, Inc., 1980) p 145.
5. 'Twelve Steps in the Grief Process'. Theos National Headquarters, Pensylvania 15222.
6. Henri Nouwen, *The Inner Voice of Love* (London: Darton, Longman & Todd, 1997) p 32.
7. Psalm 139:23,24
8. Psalm 139:13,16
9. Mark 9:23

10. Philippians 4:13
11. Viktor Frankl, *Man's Search for Meaning* (Beacon Press, 1993).
12. Deuteronomy 23:5
13. 2 Corinthians 1:4

Chapter Five
1. Stephen R. Covey, *The Seven Habits of Highly Effective People* (Hemel Hempstead: Simon & Schuster Ltd., 1989) p 108.
2. John Powell, *Happiness is an Inside Job* (T. More Press, 1996).
3. David Cormack, *Change Directions* (Crowborough, Monarch Pub) p 205.
4. Stephen R. Covey, *The Seven Habits of Highly Effective People, op. cit.* p 71.
5. Abe Wagner, *Say It Straight or You Will Show it Crooked* (Industrial Society, 1986) p 119.
6. Ibid, p 118.
7. Stephen Covey, *The Seven Habits of Highly Effective People,* op. cit. p 43.
8. Ibid, p 71.
9. Abe Wagner, *Say It Straight or You Will Show it Crooked,* op. cit. p 81.

Chapter Six
1. Chris Spicer, *Eight Characteristics of Highly Effective Christians* (London: Monarch, 1996).
2. George New & David Cormack, *Why Did I Do That?* (London: Hodder & Stoughton, 1997) p 24.
3. Proverbs 16:2
4. Proverbs 20:5
5. Dr Richard L. Ganz, *The Secret of Self-Control* (Leicester: Crossway Books, 1989) p 86.
6. Psalm 42:5
7. 1 Corinthians 4:5
8. 1 Thessalonians 2:3
9. James 4:3
10. Jeremiah 2:13
11. Stephen Covey, *The Seven Habits of Highly Effective People* (Hemel Hempstead: Simon and Schuster, 1989) p 157.

12. Matthew 6:1
13. Numbers 12:3
14. Genesis 50:20
15. Dr Richard L. Ganz, *The Secret of Self-Control*, op. cit. p 135.
16. Luke 2:49
17. John 5:19
18. John 6:38
19. Luke 22:42
20. Matthew 6:9
21. *Stories For the Heart*, compiled by Alice Gray (Questar Publishers, 1996) p 105.
22. Ibid, p 112.
23. Chris Spicer, *Eight Characteristics of Highly Effective Christians*, op. cit. p 153.
24. Richard Dortch, *Integrity* (New Leaf Press, 1992) p 87.
25. Ibid, p 311.
26. Matthew 6:33
27. Proverbs 11:21 (TLB)
28. Barbara Johnson, *Splashes of Joy in the Cesspools of Life* (Milton Keynes: Word Publishing, 1992) p 176.
29. Ibid, p 177.
30. Victor Frankl, *Man's Search for Meaning* (Beacon Press, 1993).
31. Stephen Covey, *The Seven Habits of Highly Effective People*, op. cit. p 98.
32. Carol Wimber, *John Wimber: The Way it Was* (London: Hodder & Stoughton, 1999) p 214.
33. John Maxwell, *Developing the Leader Within You* (Milton Keynes: Thomas Nelson, 1993) p 161.
34. Sister Sesharatnamma, *A Pathway to Heaven* (Kansas City: Grace Ministries).

Chapter Seven

1. Dr Derek Morphew, *Breakthrough* (Vineyard Int. Pub., 1991) p 59.
2. Carol Wimber, *John Wimber, The Way it Was* (London: Hodder & Stoughton, 1999) p 109.
3. Ibid, p 49
4. Matthew 12:28
5. Matthew 4:17

6. Matthew 10:7,8
7. Matthew 25:1–13
8. Dr Derek Morphew, *Breakthrough,* op. cit. p 135.
9. Mark 13:10
10. Revelation 21:3,4
11. Carol Wimber, *John Wimber, The Way it Was,* op. cit. p 108.
12. Matthew 10:29,30
13. Catherine Marshall, *Something More* (London: Hodder & Stoughton, 1974).
14. John Powell, *The Christian Vision* (T. More Press, 1996).
15. Genesis 3:16–19
16. Romans 8:28
17. Ephesians 1:11
18. Matthew 16:24
19. Romans 5:3
20. James 1:2–4
21. Hebrews 5:8; 2:10
22. *The Stories of Life,* retold by Alice Gray (Questar Pub., 1996) p 212.
23. 2 Corinthians 12:9
24. Hosea 2:15
25. Isaiah 53:3,10
26. 2 Corinthians 1:3,4
27. Romans 8:35–39
28. Romans 8:18
29. Hebrews 12:2

Chapter Eight

1. Ecclesiastes 3:1,4
2. Barbara Johnson, *Splashes of Joy in the Cesspools of Life* (Milton Keynes: Word Pub., 1992) p 39.
3. Os Guinness, *God In The Darkness* (London: Hodder & Stoughton, 1996) p 181.
4. Matthew 26:36–40
5. 2 Samuel 1:25
6. Psalm 6:3
7. Psalm 13:1,2
8. 2 Corinthians 6:3–4
9. 2 Corinthians 6:8-10

10　Richard Wurmbrand, *In God's Underground* (W.H. Allen, 1968).

11. 2 Corinthians 4:18

12. Barbara Johnson, *Splashes of Joy in the Cesspools of Life,* op. cit. p 61.

13. Habakkuk 1:2,3

14. Habakkuk 2:4

15. Job 31:35; 38:2; 42:2

16. Deuteronomy 23:5

17. Os Guinness, *God in the Dark,* op. cit. p 178.

18. John 14:9

19. *The God I Don't Believe In* (Abbey Press, 1973). Quoted in: *The Christian Vision,* John Powell (T. More Press, 1996).

Chapter Nine

1. Hebrews 11:8

2. Habakkuk 3:17–18

3. 2 Corinthians 2:1

4. Os Guinness, *God In The Dark* (London: Hodder & Stoughton, 1996) p 180.

5. Matthew 26:26

6. 1 Thessalonians 5:16–18

7. Ephesians 5:20

8. Catherine Marshall, *Something More* (London: Hodder & Stoughton, 1974) p 15.

9. 1 Thessalonians 5:16–18

10. F.W. Bourne, *The King's Son* (Epworth Press, 1877) p 41.

11. Proverbs 17:22

12. Abe Wagner, *Say It Straight or You'll Show It Crooked* (Industrial Society, 1996) p 123.

13. Daniel Goleman, *Emotional Intelligence* (London: Bantam Books, 1995) p 85,87.

14. Colossians 3:16

15. Charles M. Irish, *Back to the Upper Room* (Milton Keynes: Thomas Nelson Pub., 1993) p 105.

16. Psalm 30:11

17. 1 Corinthians 15:57

18. 2 Corinthians 2:14

19. 2 Corinthians 9:15

20. Hebrews 13:15
21. F.W. Bourne, *The King's Son,* op. cit. p 90.
22. Hebrews 13:15
23. Barbara Johnson, *Splashes of Joy in the Cesspool of Life* (Milton Keynes: Word Publishing, 1992) p 58.
24. *Stories For the Heart,* compiled by Alice Gray (Oregon: Multnomah Books,1996) p 88.
25. Daniel 6:7–10
26. Deuteronomy 28:47,48

Chapter Ten
1. Proverbs 15:13
2. Psalm 37:4
3. Philippians 4:6
4. Philippians 4:11–14
5. 'A Picture of Peace' by Catherine Marshall, in *Stories of the Heart,* compiled by Alice Gray (Oregon: Multnomah Books, 1996) p 239.
6. Colossians 3:15
7. Leslie Weatherhead, *Prescription for Anxiety* (London: Hodder & Stoughton, 1956) p 104.
8. Barbara Johnson, *Splashes of Joy in the Cesspools of Life* (Milton Keynes: Word Pub., 1992) p 18.
9. F.W.Bourne, *The King's Son* (Epworth Press, 1877).
10. Carol Wimber, *John Wimber: The Way it Was* (London: Hodder & Stoughton, 1999) p 206.
11. 2 Chronicles 5:12–14
12. Psalm 22:3 (KJV)
13. Ephesians 1:12
14. 2 Chronicles 20:14–22
15. Acts 16:16–34
16. Helen H. Lemmel, copyright © 1922; renewal 1950 by H.H. Lemmel, Singspiration, a division of Zondervan.

New Wine Vision

We want to see as many Christians and Churches as possible alive with the joy of knowing and worshipping Jesus Christ, and equipped to live out and proclaim his Kingdom in the love of God the Father, and the power and gifts of the Holy Spirit.

New Wine Mission

Through the Holy Spirit, we seek fulfilment of this vision through:

* Summer Family Conferences. These events aim to envision and empower Christians and Churches for worship which is passionate, intimate, reverent and biblical; for ministry in the power and gifts of the Spirit, modelled in a mature, responsible way; and through Bible expositions and a breadth of seminar options, to equip them for Spirit-filled Christian life and ministry.

* The work of the New Wine Networks. Providing relational support and encouragement for like minded leaders across the UK and other nations. Regional training conferences (1-3 days in length) are held all around the networks. We also place strategic emphasis on training church leaders through a programme of leadership training conferences, and the New Wine Leaders' Retreats.

* Encouraging faith-sharing visits to churches that are seeking to grow in renewal by leaders and other teachers taking out teams of people from their churches

* Discerning where the Spirit is leading in issues of social responsibility, justice, community and the environment.

* Encouraging Church Planting.

* Publishing: New Wine Magazine, books and other teaching materials (e.g. video and audio cassette material) as a further means of propagating teaching which adheres to New Wine values.

In this work we have an especial, though not exclusive, concern for the Church of England, from which New Wine emerged, and other traditional Churches.

New Wine – equipping churches to extend Jesus' Kingdom

New Wine. 4A Ridley Avenue, Ealing, London W13 9XW
Tel. 020 8567 6717   Fax. 020 8840 4735
Email info@new-wine.org   Web Site www.new-wine.org